MAY 2 8 2004
MORENO VALLEY

D0502989

MVFOL

AN INSIDER'S GUIDE TO THE UN

AN INSIDER'S GUIDE

TO

THE

UN

LINDA FASULO

Yale University Press / New Haven and London

Moreno Valley Public Library

Copyright © 2004 by Linda Fasulo. All rights reserved. This book may not be reproduced, in whole or in part, including illustrations, in any form (beyond that copying permitted by Sections 107 and 108 of the U.S. Copyright Law and except by reviewers for the public press), without written permission from the publishers.

Set in Scala type by Keystone Typesetting, Inc. Printed in the United States of America by Vail-Ballou Press.

Library of Congress Cataloging-in-Publication Data
Fasulo, Linda M.
An insider's guide to the UN / Linda Fasulo.
    p.   cm.
Includes bibliographical references and index.
ISBN 0-300-10155-4 (cloth : alk. paper)
ISBN 0-300-10154-6 (pbk. : alk. paper)
1. United Nations—Popular works. I. Title.
JZ4984.6.F37 2003
341.23—dc21   2003010668

A catalogue record for this book is available from the British Library.

The paper in this book meets the guidelines for permanence and durability of the Committee on Production Guidelines for Book Longevity of the Council on Library Resources.

10 9 8 7 6 5 4 3 2

For my son, Alex, my husband, Robert, and my mother, Mary

CONTENTS

ACKNOWLEDGMENTS

This book would not have been possible without the encouragement, advice, and support of many people. To all the diplomats, UN officials, analysts, and observers whom I have interviewed, I express my thanks for their interest in this project. This especially includes Ambassador Richard Holbrooke, David Malone, Mark Malloch Brown, Ambassador John Negroponte, Shepard Forman, Ambassador Nancy Soderberg, Ambassador Danilo Turk, Secretary of State Madeleine Albright, Michael Sheehan, and Shashi Tharoor, who all graciously shared their unique and invaluable personal insights.

For their generous financial support, I'm very grateful to the UN Foundation and the Better World Campaign, in particular Melinda Kimble and Phyllis Cuttino. I also thank the Rockefeller Brothers Fund, specifically its president Stephen Heintz, for helping to fund the project. In addition, I thank the World Affairs Council of Philadelphia, especially its president, Buntzie Ellis Churchill, and Claudia McBride and Margaret Lonzetta for their enthusiastic sponsorship.

Warm thanks go to Kirsten Plonner, my researcher, for her devoted day-to-day work in seeing this book to completion, and to longtime friend and colleague Bill Zeisel of QED Associates for his discerning eye in the preparation of the manuscript. I thank my son Alex for his technical savvy and research assistance, and my friend Esther Margolis for introducing me to Yale University Press. I'm grateful to have had the opportunity to work with the wonderful staff at Yale University Press, particularly senior editor John Kulka and manuscript editor Nancy Moore.

I also express appreciation to my friends and colleagues at the UN, NBC News, and National Public Radio who gave encouragement along the way. And throughout this experience, my family has been remarkably patient and supportive. For this I am extremely grateful.

Working as a news correspondent at the United Nations has given me a first-hand perspective on one of the world's finest and most important governing bodies. Nowhere else in the world can you watch an international group of luminaries discuss the great issues of our day and make decisions that can define our lives for years to come. Curbing international terrorism, combating diseases like malaria and AIDS, and trying to bring rogue nations like North Korea to account are only a few of the big problems the UN can address in a year.

At the UN, before the proceedings begin the agenda has been set, the members have prepared themselves, confrontations have played out in relative privacy, and the public sees a polished performance. Many onlookers will accept this performance at face value and never give it another thought. For those who want to know more, who ask how the proceedings are conceived, prepared, and paid for, and about their chances for a lasting impact, I have written this book, relying on my personal observations as well as the experiences and insights of other insiders. Just as I was about to start writing, however, the world changed forever.

President George W. Bush speaks at a luncheon hosted by UN Secretary General Kofi Annan for world leaders attending a General Assembly meeting on terrorism, Nov. 10, 2001. UN/DPI photo by Eskinder Debebe.

The book would have been different if I had written it before 9/11. It would have devoted much more space to discussing the effectiveness of the UN and whether it serves American interests. It would have argued more extensively for the importance of globalization as a force that has woven the United States into the world fabric so tightly and in so many ways that we can no longer fantasize about "going it alone." It might even have dwelled on the need to keep the UN based in New York City rather than move it to another world capital as some have suggested. All these points are now moot.

The terrorist attacks in New York City and Washington, D.C., have changed many things, not least how the United States sees the United Nations. The media have begun to focus on the UN as a key ally in the fight against international terrorism. The UN has become more favored as a partner of the world's sole superpower. Americans have begun regarding the UN with renewed hope and interest, asking if it can transcend its old reputation for shortcomings. The insiders who

The UN was officially established on Oct. 24, 1945, when the UN Charter was ratified. Thus October 24 is celebrated every year as UN Day. President Franklin D. Roosevelt coined the name "United Nations," first used in the "Declaration by United Nations" on January 1, 1942.

run the UN and its associated agencies, and the diplomats who represent its member nations, have been asking similar questions. Most believe it will step up to the new challenges, but that is by no means the unanimous view.

More than half a century ago, the United States and its allies in World War II created an international body that they hoped would enable nations to prosper and live peacefully with one another. When the war ended in 1945, the new organization began with enormous goodwill, moral support from all sides, and strong US leadership. The world waited to see if the UN could rectify the shortcomings of the League of Nations, its predecessor organization, which dissolved in the late 1930s, victim of totalitarian regimes and US indifference. Could it be the uniting force among the victorious nations, whose ideologies and political interests often seemed at odds?

The cold war soon replaced idealistic collaboration with power politics between the West and the East. From the late 1940s until the breakup of the Soviet Union in 1991, confrontation among the blocs defined most UN relationships, discussions, debates, programs, and activities. A whole generation grew up with an East–West mindset, whose ghost still surfaces at the UN and elsewhere, even though the old blocs are gone and a new world is gradually emerging. During these many decades, expectations about the UN changed, becoming either more realistic or more cynical, depending on the viewpoint.

Today, although Americans do not expect the UN to solve all the world's problems, at the least we would like it to be a more effective partner in dealing with the forces that are transforming our world. These forces include international terrorism and much more. Economic forces are spinning new webs of relations among nations.

"People [at the UN] acknowledge and recognize our importance and want to find ways to work more closely with us. They don't necessarily want to write us a blank check or do something that they perceive to be writing the United States a blank check, but they go to considerable lengths to work with us."—John Negroponte, US Ambassador to the UN

Public opinion is becoming something that many governments have to reckon with, as citizens connect with the world and become more affluent, educated, and willing to stand up for their rights. Changes in the natural environment are presenting challenges that can be solved only through international cooperation. Even the notion of human rights has changed, largely owing to the successful efforts of bodies like the UN to create and publicize international standards of behavior. What constitutes a threat to peace and security has broadened, to include dangers as diverse as AIDS, rights abuses, drug trafficking, and money laundering. We are less willing than before to let cultural difference excuse rights abuses, if only because nearly all nations have signed treaties that outlaw such abuses.

In the face of such rapid and wrenching change, we have to wonder how an organization created nearly sixty years ago, in a very different world, could possibly be relevant today, let alone in the future. That is the UN's greatest challenge—one it is addressing by trying to focus more on "the people" than on governments. Although the UN was created and still functions largely as an organization composed of government representatives, it is reaching out directly to the people in various ways. If this effort succeeds, the UN will become quite a different kind of organization.

This new emphasis on the people highlights the importance of the human factor in institutions like the United Nations. As one of my "insiders" says, people really do matter at the UN, and they act in a context full of illusion, opinion, perception, and emotion. In order to provide some understanding of that context, this book begins by exploring some basic aspects of the UN, such as how it came into existence and the governing principles that guide its operation.

ACABQ—Advisory Committee on Administrative and Budgetary
   Questions
ACUNS—Academic Council on the United Nations System
ASIL—American Society for International Law
BCUN—Business Council for the United Nations
CEDAW—Convention on the Elimination of All Forms of
   Discrimination Against Women
CND—Commission on Narcotic Drugs
CONGO—Conference on Non-Governmental Organizations in
   Consultative Status
CRC—Convention on the Rights of the Child
CTBTO—Preparatory Commission for the Comprehensive Nuclear-
   Test-Ban Treaty Organization
DPA—Department of Political Affairs
DPI—Department of Public Information
DPKO—Department of Peacekeeping Operations
E-10—Elected 10 members of the Security Council
ECOSOC—Economic and Social Council
ECOWAS—Economic Council of West African States

ETTA—East Timor Transitional Administration
EU—European Union
FAO—Food and Agriculture Organization
G-77—A coalition of developing countries
GA—General Assembly
GAO—General Accounting Office
GATT—General Agreement on Tariffs and Trade
HCHR—High Commissioner for Human Rights
IAEA—International Atomic Energy Agency
ICAO—International Civil Aviation Organization
ICC—International Criminal Court
ICCPR—International Covenant on Civil and Political Rights
ICJ—International Court of Justice
ICTR—International Criminal Tribunal for Rwanda
ICTY—International Criminal Tribunal for (the former) Yugoslavia
IDA—International Development Association
IFAD—International Fund for Agricultural Development
ILO—International Labor Organization
IMF—International Monetary Fund
IMO—International Maritime Organization
INSTRAW—International Research and Training Institute for the
    Advancement of Women
IPCC—Intergovernmental Panel on Climate Change
ISA—International Studies Association
ITU—International Telecommunications Union
NAM—Nonaligned Movement
NATO—North Atlantic Treaty Organization
NGO—nongovernmental organization
OAU—Organization of African Unity
OEWG—Open-Ended Working Group on the Question of Equitable
    Representation on and Increase in the Membership of the Security
    Council
OHCHR—Office of the High Commissioner for Human Rights
OIOS—Office of Internal Oversight Services
OPCW—Organization for the Prohibition of Chemical Weapons

P5—Permanent 5 members of the Security Council
PCT—Patent Cooperation Treaty
PR—A Nation's Permanent Representative or Perm Rep
SC—Security Council
SG—Secretary General
UN—United Nations
UNA-USA—United Nations Association of the United States of
    America
UNAIDS—Joint United Nations Program on HIV/AIDS
UNCTAD—UN Conference on Trade and Development
UNDCP—UN International Drug Control Program
UNDP—United Nations Development Program
UNEP—United Nations Environment Program
UNESCO—United Nations Educational, Scientific, and Cultural
    Organization
UNF—United Nations Foundation
UNFPA—United Nations Population Fund
UNHCR—Office of the United Nations High Commissioner for
    Refugees
UNICEF—United Nations Children's Fund
UNIDO—UN Industrial Development Organization
UNIFEM—UN Development Fund for Women
UNMEE—UN Mission in Ethiopia and Eritrea
UNMOVIC—United Nations Monitoring, Verification, and
    Inspection Commission on Iraq
UNODC—United Nations Office on Drugs and Crime
UNOPS—UN Office for Project Services
UPU—Universal Postal Union
UNRWA—United Nations Relief and Works Agency for Palestine
    Refugees in the Near East
UNSCOM—United Nations Special Commission on Iraq
UNTAET—UN Transitional Administration in East Timor
UNTSO—United Nations Truce Supervision Organization
UNV—UN Volunteers
UPU—Universal Postal Union

WEOG—Western Europe and Others bloc
WFP—World Food Program
WHO—World Health Organization
WIPO—World Intellectual Property Organization
WMO—World Meteorological Organization

AN INSIDER'S GUIDE TO THE UN

CHAPTER 1

An Overview

As the Charter makes clear, the United Nations was intended to introduce new principles into international relations, making a qualitative difference to their day-to-day conduct. The Charter's very first Article defines our purposes: resolving disputes by peaceful means; devising cooperative solutions to economic, social, cultural and humanitarian problems; and broadly encouraging behavior in conformity with the principles of justice and international law.

—Kofi Annan, Secretary General of the United Nations

The UN came into existence as a result of the most terrible war in history. During World War II, American President Franklin Roosevelt, British Prime Minister Winston Churchill, and the leaders of several other major combatant nations agreed that it was necessary to create a world organization that would help ensure the peace in future years. Their ideas are enshrined in the Preamble to the UN's Charter, which is one of its fundamental documents:

> *We the peoples of the United Nations determined*
> to save succeeding generations from the scourge of war, which twice in our lifetime has brought untold sorrow to mankind, and

Josef Stalin, Franklin Roosevelt, and Winston Churchill meet at the Yalta Conference in Yalta, USSR, Feb. 12, 1945. UN/DPI photo.

to reaffirm faith in fundamental human rights, in the dignity and worth of the human person, in the equal rights of men and women and of nations large and small, and

to establish conditions under which justice and respect for the obligations arising from treaties and other sources of international law can be maintained, and

to promote social progress and better standards of life in larger freedom,

and for these ends

to practice tolerance and live together in peace with one another as good neighbors, and

to unite our strength to maintain international peace and security, and

to ensure, by the acceptance of principles and the institution of methods, that armed force shall not be used, save in the common interest, and

to employ international machinery for the promotion of the economic and social advancement of all peoples,

have resolved to combine our efforts to accomplish these aims
Accordingly, our respective Governments, through representatives
assembled in the city of San Francisco, who have exhibited their
full powers found to be in good and due form, have agreed to the
present Charter of the United Nations and do hereby establish an
international organization to be known as the United Nations.

As the Preamble declares, the world's peoples, acting through their
representatives, seek to create a just and prosperous world through
common action. It could hardly be simpler, and yet during more than
half a century of trying we still live amid global insecurity and, in
many places, injustice and suffering. And the UN itself is far from
simple. It straddles the globe, operating in almost every nation on
earth, and has a bewildering variety of offices, programs, and personnel. Let's begin, then, with some basic points and language that will
appear throughout the book.

What Is the United Nations?

One of the points is that the UN is not always what it seems to be.
Consider the following: many people, if asked to define the UN, would
probably respond that it is a large organization devoted to world peace,
and that it has several main bodies, such as the General Assembly and
the Security Council, and an executive leader, the Secretary General. It
is headquartered in New York City, they would say, but has operations
all over the world.

A look at the UN's organizational flowchart largely confirms this
general picture. At the top are the six principal organs (see Appendix
A), some of which are household names: the International Court of
Justice (better known as the World Court), the Security Council (where
five selected countries have the right to veto any resolution they don't
like), the General Assembly (which consists of delegates from all
member nations of the UN), the Economic and Social Council, the
Trusteeship Council (which did its job so well it has lost its reason for
being), and the Secretariat (whose director, Kofi Annan, is a global

diplomat-superstar). With the exception of the Trusteeship Council, these principal organs get the most media coverage and are, in some ways, the most significant movers and shakers within the UN (see Appendix A for a breakdown of UN groups).

When we move to the second tier of organizations, the scene is more complicated. Here we find an amazing collection of entities and organizations, some of which are actually older than the UN itself and operate with almost complete independence from it. Best known to the public are the "Specialized Agencies," such as the United Nations Educational, Scientific, and Cultural Organization (UNESCO), the World Health Organization (WHO), the World Bank, and the International Monetary Fund (IMF). Another group, called "Programs and Funds," includes one very well known body, the United Nations Children's Fund (UNICEF), and several others that appear frequently in the news, like the United Nations Environment Program (which considers global warming and other environmental issues) and the United Nations High Commissioner for Refugees (UNHCR). Below them on the chart are "Other UN Entities," featuring one standout, the Human Rights Commission, which meets in Geneva and receives enormous press coverage, and three others that play important but less publicized roles. The five research institutes likewise keep a low public profile.

The "related organizations" are a unique group because they contain two entities with the same acronym (bad planning!): the World Trade Organization, which almost everyone has heard of, and the World Tourism Organization, which almost no one has heard of except tourism professionals. Above them are two sets of commissions. The "Functional Commissions" include some that on first glance seem to poach on the ground of other entities. For example, the Commission on Narcotic Drugs seems to overlap the UN Drug Control Program, on the left side of the chart. Similarly, the Commission on the Status of Women seems to overlap the UN Development Fund for Women. However, the overlap is more apparent than real in these two cases, because the Functional Commissions concentrate on policy while the agencies are oriented more toward implementation. Now, if there are "Functional Commissions," you might expect to find "Dysfunctional Commissions" too (and their existence has been asserted by some critics). Instead we find the "Regional Commissions," which are among the least known of UN bodies. They set policy about economic development in the regions of Africa, Europe, Latin America and the Caribbean, Asia and the Pacific, and Western Asia.

The position of the supporting organizations on the flowchart does not make them merely adjuncts of the entities above them. To the contrary, many of them run their own affairs with little interference and, as critics have complained, with not much communication with the peer agencies, programs, or commissions with which they share interests.

We now have a good schematic picture of the UN's structure. But this is only a beginning. When we think about these organizations in action, flowcharts aren't very helpful. They don't answer simple questions like whether the UN has a military establishment or whether it can raise taxes. Nor does it help to ask the people around you, because polls have revealed that while most Americans have a pretty friendly view of the UN, they know little about even its basic workings, and often attribute to it powers and authority it doesn't have. Richard Holbrooke, the US Ambassador to the UN during the last two years of the Clinton administration, has a reputation for toughness and a penchant for aggressively pushing the American viewpoint. He tells a story about a recent speaking engagement in Odessa, Texas—"George Bush country," as he puts it—when "some guy asked 'What do you think about this world government thing?' I said there was no such thing, and he said, 'What about the UN, that's a world government, they are trying to take away our liberties.' And I said, 'Well, Sir, that is just not true.' There are people out there who think the UN has that kind of power and insidious influence, and the truth is the exact opposite, the UN is too weak, not too strong. You start with a certain percentage of people completely misunderstanding the UN, criticizing it from the wrong point of view. Too strong is their fear when in fact too weak to be effective is the truth."

THE UNITED NATIONS SYSTEM

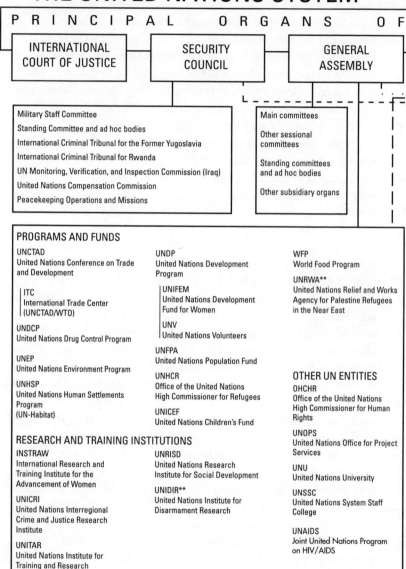

PRINCIPAL ORGANS OF

INTERNATIONAL COURT OF JUSTICE	SECURITY COUNCIL	GENERAL ASSEMBLY

Military Staff Committee

Standing Committee and ad hoc bodies

International Criminal Tribunal for the Former Yugoslavia

International Criminal Tribunal for Rwanda

UN Monitoring, Verification, and Inspection Commission (Iraq)

United Nations Compensation Commission

Peacekeeping Operations and Missions

Main committees

Other sessional committees

Standing committees and ad hoc bodies

Other subsidiary organs

PROGRAMS AND FUNDS

UNCTAD
United Nations Conference on Trade and Development

| ITC
International Trade Center
(UNCTAD/WTO)

UNDCP
United Nations Drug Control Program

UNEP
United Nations Environment Program

UNHSP
United Nations Human Settlements Program
(UN-Habitat)

UNDP
United Nations Development Program

| UNIFEM
United Nations Development Fund for Women

UNV
United Nations Volunteers

UNFPA
United Nations Population Fund

UNHCR
Office of the United Nations High Commissioner for Refugees

UNICEF
United Nations Children's Fund

WFP
World Food Program

UNRWA**
United Nations Relief and Works Agency for Palestine Refugees in the Near East

OTHER UN ENTITIES

OHCHR
Office of the United Nations High Commissioner for Human Rights

UNOPS
United Nations Office for Project Services

UNU
United Nations University

UNSSC
United Nations System Staff College

UNAIDS
Joint United Nations Program on HIV/AIDS

RESEARCH AND TRAINING INSTITUTIONS

INSTRAW
International Research and Training Institute for the Advancement of Women

UNICRI
United Nations Interregional Crime and Justice Research Institute

UNITAR
United Nations Institute for Training and Research

UNRISD
United Nations Research Institute for Social Development

UNIDIR**
United Nations Institute for Disarmament Research

* Autonomous organizations working with the United Nations and each other through the coordinating machinery of the Economic and Social Council.

** Report only to the General Assembly.

Published by the United Nations Department of Public Information DPI/2299–February 2003.

THE UNITED NATIONS

ECONOMIC AND SOCIAL COUNCIL	TRUSTEESHIP COUNCIL	SECRETARIAT

FUNCTIONAL COMMISSIONS

Commission for Social Development
Commission on Human Rights
Commission on Narcotic Drugs
Commission on Crime Prevention and Criminal Justice
Commission on Science and Technology for Development
Commission on Sustainable Development
Commission on the Status of Women
Commission on Population and Development
Statistical Commission

REGIONAL COMMISSIONS

Economic Commission for Africa (ECA)
Economic Commission for Europe (ECE)
Economic Commission for Latin America and the Caribbean (ECLAC)
Economic Commission for Asia and the Pacific (ESCAP)
Economic Commission for Western Asia (ESCWA)
United Nations Forum on Forestry
Sessional and Standing Committees Expert, ad hoc, and related bodies

RELATED ORGANIZATIONS

IAEA
International Atomic Energy Agency

WTO (trade)
World Trade Organization

WTO (tourism)
World Tourism Organization

CTBTO
Preparatory Commission for the Comprehensive Nuclear-Test-Ban-Treaty Organization

OPCW
Organization for the Prohibition of Chemical Weapons

SPECIALIZED AGENCIES*

ILO
International Labor Organization

FAO
Food and Agriculture Organization of the United Nations

UNESCO
United Nations Educational, Scientific, and Cultural Organization

WHO
World Health Organization

WORLD BANK GROUP

IBRD	International Bank for Reconstruction and Development
IDA	International Development Association
IFC	International Finance Corporation
MIG	Multilateral Investment Guarantee Agency
ICSID	International Center for Settlement of Investment disputes

IMF
International Monetary Fund

ICAO
International Civil Aviation Organization

IMO
International Maritime Organization

ITU
International Telecommunications Union

UPU
Universal Postal Union

WMO
World Meteorological Organization

WIPO
World Intellectual Property Organization

IFAD
International Fund for Agricultural Development

UNIDO
United Nations Industrial Development Organization

SECRETARIAT

OSG
Office of the Secretary-General

OIOS
Office of Internal Oversight Services

OLA
Office of Legal Affairs

DPA
Department of Political Affairs

DDA
Department for Disarmament Affairs

DPKO
Department of Peacekeeping Operations

OCHA
Office for the Coordination of Humanitarian Affairs

DESA
Department of Economic and Social Affairs

DGAACS
Department of General Assembly Affairs and Conference Services

DPI
Department of Public Information

DM
Department of Management

OIP
Office of the Iraq Program

UNSECOORD
Office of the United Nations Security Coordinator

ODC
Office on Drugs and Crime

UNOG
UN Office at Geneva

UNOV
UN Office at Vienna

UNON
UN Office at Nairobi

The Trusteeship Council

Of the six principal organs of the UN, the Trusteeship Council is easily the least well known, and for good reason. On Nov. 1, 1994, it suspended operations and ceased to exist except on paper. How can it be that one of the UN's original working parts should no longer be considered necessary? The demise of the council is part of the very successful role the UN has played in decolonization, the process by which some eighty nations have come into existence, since 1945. When decolonization began, most of Africa was controlled by a few Western nations, mainly the UK, France, and Belgium, while the Netherlands, UK, and France ruled large parts of Asia, including Indonesia, India, Pakistan, and Vietnam. Japan had ruled Korea for half a century, and the United States had just acquired, through military conquest, control of many Pacific islands such as the Marshalls. Many of the colonized peoples sought independence, and soon the world's colonial empires were being swept away or voluntarily relinquished. Sentiment against colonialism mounted quickly in the UN, which encouraged the move to independence.

Scattered around the world were territories, like Papua, New Guinea, and the Mariana Islands in the Pacific, that had been wards of the League of Nations and were now administered by Australia, the US, and other nations. Article 75 of the Charter states that "the United Nations shall establish under its authority an international trusteeship system for the administration and supervision of such territories as may be placed thereunder by subsequent individual agreements. These territories are hereinafter referred to as trust territories." The UN wanted to ensure that trustee nations would truly look after the best interests of their charges and help them secure self-government, either on their own or as parts of larger entities. To guarantee that they received adequate attention, the Trusteeship Council was composed of the five permanent members of the Security Council. Palau, an island group in the Pacific, was the last UN trust territory. During World War II, the US occupied Palau, which had been under the trusteeship of Japan through the League of Nations. Palau became a UN member on Dec. 15, 1994.

The UN Cast

The UN is made up of Six Principal Organs, all based in New York City except the ICJ, which is based in The Hague:

Secretariat

Security Council

General Assembly

International Court of Justice (ICJ)

Trusteeship Council (no longer meets)

Economic and Social Council

—Plus UN programs and funds, which are essential to working for development, humanitarian assistance, and human rights. They include the UN Children's Fund (UNICEF), the UN Development Program (UNDP), and the Office of the United Nations High Commissioner for Refugees (UNHCR).

—Plus the UN specialized agencies, which coordinate their work with the UN but are separate organizations. Agencies, such as the International Monetary Fund, the World Health Organization (WHO), and the International Civil Aviation Organization, focus on specific areas.

—Plus thousands of nongovernmental organizations (NGOs) that are independent citizens' organizations associated with the UN. They are concerned with many of the same issues as the UN, such as human rights, arms control, and the environment. NGOs are not part of the UN but have become important to its functioning in many key areas.

The UN's New York City headquarters is considered international territory.

One former US Ambassador to the UN, Nancy Soderberg, claims that "there is no such single thing as the UN." Rather, the UN "is 191 countries with different agendas and a whole collection of civil servants who work there, and it's all Jell-O. You can't say what the UN is because you touch one area and it comes out looking differently on the other side." According to Michael Sheehan, an American who

Michael Sheehan was UN Assistant Secretary General for Peacekeeping, 2001–3. A former US Army officer, he was Ambassador-at-Large and Coordinator for Counter Terrorism in the US State Department, and before that served in the Clinton White House on the staff of the National Security Council, as director of International Organizations and Peacekeeping. In 2003 Sheehan was appointed Deputy Commissioner of Counter Terrorism in the New York City Police Department.

served in the UN's peacekeeping department, "the UN is an organization that has enormous talent, but often its mandates are so obtuse that its actual ability to function is limited." It may be blamed for failing to meet goals for which its members—the world's nations— don't give it sufficient resources.

Yet, can we ignore it? The United States does not have the choice of acting "only through the UN or only alone," says former Secretary of State Madeleine Albright. "We want—and need—both options. So in diplomacy, an instrument like the UN will be useful in some situations, useless in others, and extremely valuable in getting the whole job done." The UN can help make the world a better place, which is to our advantage because we know that "desperation is a parent to violence, that democratic principles are often among the victims of poverty and that lawlessness is a contagious disease." Albright has stated it neatly: "We cannot be the world's policemen, though we're very good at it."

UN and US: Perfect Together?

Insiders agree that just as the United States needs the UN, the United Nations needs the US. "I need to underscore repeatedly that the UN is only as good as the US commitment," says Richard Holbrooke, who negotiated the Dayton Accords that ended the war in Bosnia in 1995. The United States is such a vast global presence that its support is essential for success: "The UN cannot succeed if the US does not support it."

In 1999 Mark Malloch Brown became the Administrator of the UN
Development Program, a post to which he was reappointed in 2003
for a second four-year term. He chairs the UN Development Group,
a committee of the heads of all UN development funds, programs,
and departments. From 1994–99 he served at the World Bank. He
founded the *Economist Development Report* and served as its editor
from 1983–86. He is a British citizen, educated in Great Britain and
the United States.

Unfortunately, many insiders say, the US has usually been unable
to find and follow a clear, consistent policy toward the UN. Mark
Malloch Brown, Administrator of the United Nations Development
Program (UNDP) and highly regarded by his American peers, sees a
"bewildered superpower, self-confident at home, uneasy abroad . . .
and all of this comes together at the UN." One manifestation of the
US government's ambivalence has been its reluctance to pay its dues
to the general budget of the UN and some of the subbudgets. As
described in more detail in Chapter 12, the accumulated arrears (almost $1 billion by September 2001) severely cramped the UN's ability
to operate and was the source of much friction. To be fair, however, it
should be noted that the US and some other nations have withheld
dues in varying amounts for a variety of reasons, including allegations
of mismanagement and poor allocation of funds.

Most insiders I've talked with believe that the US can generally have
as much influence as it wants in the UN. David Malone, a former
Canadian diplomat and now president of the International Peace
Academy, argues that "a strong coherent US lead at the UN is nearly
always followed by UN member states." But, "when Washington
sends mixed signals, as it is too often wont to do owing to divergent
views in Congress and the White House, then the UN may not know
what is wanted."

Michael Sheehan speaks of a love-hate relationship between the US
and the UN but doesn't see it as particularly unusual in the context of

A career Canadian Foreign Service officer, David Malone was from
1992–94 Ambassador and Deputy Permanent Representative of
Canada to the UN, where he chaired the negotiations of the UN
Special Committee on Peacekeeping Operations and the UN General
Assembly consultations on peacekeeping issues. From 1990–92, he
represented Canada on the UN's Economic and Social Council
(ECOSOC). He is president of the International Peace Academy, a
think-tank on UN issues, in New York City.

American political thought. "I think the US and the UN will always
have this difficult relationship. It's inevitable because the UN is designed to be an organization where all nations have a chance to voice
themselves."

Shepard Forman, of New York University's Center on International
Cooperation, thinks the US needs to be more trusting of its partners.
"We don't seem to trust anyone when it comes to US national security,
and therefore we are fully prepared to go it alone, and presume others
will come along and help as we need them, but we don't always need
them. Then by extension where we think there are intersects between
security and other things, narcotic trafficking, money laundering,
where we don't think other countries may see the problem the same
way or provide the degree of help to us, we will also go it alone. We've
accepted our own hubris on being a superpower, the indispensable
nation."

Shepard Forman is director of New York University's Center on International Cooperation, which he founded. Previously he was director
of the Ford Foundation's Human Rights and Governance and International Affairs programs. Trained in anthropology and economic
development, he was a faculty member at several major US univer-
sities before joining the Ford Foundation. He has written many papers, articles, and books on international affairs, development, and
public policy.

What's in It for Me?

Putting aside international diplomacy, why should Americans care about the UN? Pressed to identify a specific UN-related item or service they have encountered recently, they might mention UNICEF holiday cards. But is that all? The UN sets standards that affect us every day. "You may think that you have never benefited personally from the UN," says Madeleine Albright, "but if you have ever traveled on an international airline or shipping line, or placed a phone call overseas, or received mail from outside the country, or been thankful for an accurate weather report—then you have been served directly or indirectly by one part or another of the UN system."

What It Means to You

"I'm struck by how relevant the work that I've had to do at the UN has been to the US national security and foreign policy agenda. Part of our debate here in the US has always turned around the issue of what does the UN mean to me? My answer to any American today is it means as much as national security and foreign policy should mean to you. It is certainly very much tied into all of that."
—John Negroponte, US Ambassador to the UN

CHAPTER 2

UN Founding Documents

Article 1
All human beings are born free and equal in dignity and rights. They are endowed with reason and conscience and should act toward one another in a spirit of brotherhood.

Article 2
Everyone is entitled to all the rights and freedoms set forth in this Declaration, without distinction of any kind, such as race, color, sex, language, religion, political or other opinion, national or social origin, property, birth or other status.   —Universal Declaration of Human Rights

As with any organization that exists in this ever-changing world, the UN cannot act according to an unchanging set of rules. But it has established two very specific annotated documents to guide its members. The UN is defined by its Charter, written in 1945, which functions as the Constitution does for the United States, and by a Universal Declaration of Human Rights, which is a manifesto of human dignity and value that remains as fresh and radical now as it was when adopted in 1948 (the entire Declaration appears in Appendix B).

The Charter lays out all the major components of the organization,

A close-up of the UN Charter, with the Egyptian delegation at the June 26, 1945, San Francisco Charter ceremony in the background. UN/DPI photo.

including its director (Secretary General), its lines of authority, and the responsibilities and rights of its members—that is, of governments that constitute UN membership. The Charter was signed on June 26, 1945, by fifty nations, and the chapters and articles constitute a treaty and are legally binding on the signatories. Article 103 of the Charter stipulates that if a member state finds that its obligations under the Charter conflict with duties under "any other international agreement," they must place their Charter obligations first.

The Universal Declaration of Human Rights is the product of the UN's Commission on Human Rights, founded in 1946, which was then led by former First Lady Eleanor Roosevelt, who had an international reputation as a crusader for human rights. Under her guidance the commission drafted the Universal Declaration as a fundamental statement about rights and freedom. Resting on Enlightenment ideals

Eleanor Roosevelt displays the Universal Declaration of Human Rights
poster in November 1949. UN photo.

of human dignity, it is unique both in its breadth and in its success as
an international standard by which to identify the basic rights that
every person should enjoy. Most human rights law, and many national
constitutions, reflect its provisions. It is an inspiration to people seeking freedom and to organizations that seek to advance the cause of
freedom and justice. Unlike the Charter, the Universal Declaration is
not a treaty and its provisions therefore are not law, but it has been
largely incorporated into two international treaties that came into effect in 1976 and have been accepted by most member states: the
International Covenant on Economic, Social, and Cultural Rights and
the International Covenant on Civil and Political Rights. The UN
refers to these covenants and the Universal Declaration as the International Bill of Rights.

CHAPTER 3

The Secretary General and the Secretariat

Article 97
The Secretariat shall comprise a Secretary-General and such staff as the
Organization may require. The Secretary-General shall be appointed by
the General Assembly upon the recommendation of the Security Council.
He shall be the chief administrative officer of the Organization.

—UN Charter

According to many insiders the UN could not have appointed a
better, more effective Secretary General than Kofi Annan, who will
serve in that post until December 31, 2006. How he got the job, a
fascinating story in its own right, will be recounted in Chapter 14.
What he has accomplished since he began his first term, on January 1,
1997, is described here.

Many regard Kofi Annan as the best Secretary General ever appointed, the equal even of the legendary Dag Hammarskjöld (1953–
61). As Mark Malloch Brown puts it, "We've had a series of Secretaries
General since Hammarskjöld who were more secretaries than generals. This is the first time since then we have a Secretary General who
dwarfs his institution."

Secretaries General

1. Kofi Annan (Ghana)   1997–Present
2. Boutros Boutros-Ghali (Egypt)   1992–96
3. Javier Perez de Cuellar (Peru)   1982–91
4. Kurt Waldheim (Austria)   1972–81
5. U Thant (Burma)   1961–71
6. Dag Hammarskjöld (Sweden)   1953–61
7. Trygve Lie (Norway)   1946–52

Annan is the first rank-and-file UN staffer to become SG, having held posts with several agencies, including the World Health Organization and the Office of the UN High Commissioner for Refugees, before becoming Undersecretary General for Peacekeeping from 1993 through 1996. Annan was born in Ghana in 1938, the son of a hereditary chief of the Fante people who was also the elected provincial governor. He grew up in an environment steeped in politics,

Secretary General Dag Hammarskjöld on a 1961 Peace Mission to the Congo, during which he was killed in a plane crash. UN photo.

which may explain his excellent interpersonal skills and his sensitivity to the views of others. As a child of the elite, the young man attended college both in his native country and in the United States (Macalester College in Minnesota), with postgraduate training at the Institute of Advanced International Studies in Geneva and also at Massachusetts Institute of Technology. Benefiting from the more activist stance the UN was able to take during the 1990s, he was soon regarded as a dynamic and resourceful leader.

Despite considerable personal modesty, and a reluctance to place himself at center stage, Annan has great presence in social settings and conveys intelligence and easy elegance. The media have covered him enthusiastically for both his charisma and his official position. His highly accomplished wife, Nane Lagergren, a Swedish lawyer and artist, is the niece of Raoul Wallenberg, who helped save many Jews from the Nazi death camps late in World War II, only to die in a Soviet prison.

Annan, Secretary General

Kofi Annan is both a media fixture and the UN official who is ultimately responsible for ensuring that members of the UN have the means and motivation to perform effectively. The Secretary General is in charge of the entire operation of the Secretariat, including policy, personnel, public relations, and long-range planning. Although the Secretariat's scope embraces almost all the significant activities of the world body, the most urgent challenges usually involve some aspect of national or international peace: making it, keeping it, or ensuring that it is not breached. In these efforts, the Secretary General works closely with the Security Council, advising the council about threats to international peace and assisting it through personal diplomacy.

In the post–cold war era, with the emergence of the United States as the dominant superpower and global peace enforcer, the Secretary General and the US President have become frequent allies in the effort to steer the world through the stresses of war, terrorism, and other threats.

The many, often conflicting responsibilities of the Secretary General

Secretary General Kofi Annan and his wife, Nane Annan, arriving in Eritrea on Dec. 8, 2000. UN/DPI photo by Jorge Aramburu.

make the post one of the most demanding imaginable. It requires intelligence and experience, certainly, but also drive, vision, and infinite tact and patience. The Secretary General must be able to communicate with the entire UN family as well as with all the nations of the world, while also administering a global array of programs and agencies.

The position of the Secretary General, only briefly described in the UN Charter, has evolved over time: "In the Charter of the UN," says Richard Holbrooke, "the role of Secretary General is only described with a single phrase, that the UN will have a chief administrative officer. It doesn't describe the authority of the Secretary General as the Constitution describes the powers for the President and Congress. It's all been done, like the British constitution, by precedent and strong Secretaries General, of whom we've had two, Dag Hammarskjöld and Kofi Annan."

Mark Malloch Brown adds that the Charter "doesn't envisage significant powers for the SG in international relations." Rather, he says, the internationally active Secretaries General have succeeded by "convincing genuinely important individuals, heads of government and so on, that they can be helpful." Michael Sheehan says that one of the Secretary General's roles is to "tell the Security Council what it has to know, not what it wants to hear. So the Secretariat is not just a puppet on a string of the member states; it has a role, and there's a dialogue between the Secretariat and the member states."

The Secretary General conducts operations through the Secretariat, consisting of approximately 8,900 staff members from about 160 countries. Most of them work in the New York City headquarters, but the Secretariat has other offices in Geneva, Vienna, and Nairobi. In keeping with the letter and spirit of the Charter, which aimed to create an international civil service, member states agree not to exert improper influence on the Secretariat's staff, and the staff, in turn, take an oath that they will be responsible solely to the United Nations and will not seek or take directions from any other authority.

Some insiders rate the staff's quality as mixed, with a few outstanding people, many good ones, and quite a few careerists who simply put in a day's work. David Malone estimates that "40 percent of the Secretariat staff are movers and shakers and carry the full burden of action. About 30 percent do no harm and do no good, and about 40 percent spend their time making trouble. Which means that the 30 percent who get work done are fairly heroic, and they exist at all levels of the system." One of the more generous evaluations comes from Nancy Soderberg, who thinks that Kofi Annan has tossed out a lot of the deadwood. "I would say that 90 percent are terrific. You have the young people who are very enthused about it and the senior people who have worked their life in the UN and loved it, and then you have a few people scattered around who are there for life. The Secretary General has very definitely moved them out over the past few years." David Malone, too, credits Annan with doing a good job of selecting first-rate people for important posts, which he rates "the most important aspect of his job" after peacekeeping.

Mark Malloch Brown makes a somewhat different criticism of the bureaucracy, citing a pervasive "disconnect between merit and

From the UN Charter, Chapter XV: The Secretariat

ARTICLE 99

The Secretary General may bring to the attention of the Security Council any matter which in his opinion may threaten the maintenance of international peace and security.

ARTICLE 100

1. In the performance of their duties the Secretary General and the staff shall not seek or receive instructions from any government or from any other authority external to the Organization. They shall refrain from any action which might reflect on their position as international officials responsible only to the Organization.
2. Each Member of the United Nations undertakes to respect the exclusively international character of the responsibilities of the Secretary General and the staff and not to seek to influence them in the discharge of their responsibilities.

ARTICLE 101

1. The staff shall be appointed by the Secretary General under regulations established by the General Assembly.
2. Appropriate staffs shall be permanently assigned to the Economic and Social Council, the Trusteeship Council, and, as required, to other organs of the United Nations. These staffs shall form a part of the Secretariat.
3. The paramount consideration in the employment of the staff and in the determination of the conditions of service shall be the necessity of securing the highest standards of efficiency, competence, and integrity. Due regard shall be paid to the importance of recruiting the staff on as wide a geographical basis as possible.

reward." He notes, "There's something rational that if you work hard and do well, you get promoted, and if you don't work hard you don't. In parts of the UN that doesn't happen." He advocates "reconnect[ing] merit to make the UN again an international meritocracy." To do this, however, Malloch Brown believes that the UN must stop promoting on the basis of political correctness that encourages hiring staff proportionately from certain regions of the world. At first glance, this might be interpreted to mean that Malloch Brown wants fewer staff from developing nations and more from the Europe–North American axis, but actually he wants just the opposite. Malloch Brown argues that Asia, Africa, and other so-called less developed regions now offer a large pool of talented, skilled, and highly motivated professionals that the UN ought to make more use of. These individuals are so highly qualified, he believes, that they will readily move up through the UN system without need of the traditional hiring quotas or the "cultural relativism which is used to promote incompetents."

Kofi Annan is ideally suited to do just what Malloch Brown urges. He knows the key UN personnel and is committed to promoting for merit. When he took office he continued and intensified an administrative overhaul begun by his predecessor, Boutros Boutros-Ghali. He has encouraged development of a corporate culture aimed at making results, not efforts, the test of effectiveness. An upshot was the creation of a new post, Deputy Secretary General of the UN, established in 1997 to help manage the Secretariat and coordinate UN programs and activities, especially those relating to economic and social development. Annan, who has sought to raise the status of women at the Secretariat, appointed Canadian Louise Fréchette to the new position.

Annan, Rights Advocate

Annan's reform efforts have generated mostly positive comment from experts, the public, and other interested observers, except in the controversial area of human rights. Everyone is "for" human rights, of course, which are enshrined in the Charter and in scores of

Louise Fréchette is the first Deputy Secretary General of the UN. A national of Canada, she assumed her duties on March 2, 1998, after having been appointed by Secretary General Kofi Annan. The Deputy Secretary General assists the Secretary General and also represents the UN at conferences and official functions. She chairs the Steering Committee on Reform and Management Policy and the Advisory Board of the UN Fund for International Partnerships (UNFIP), which handles relations with the foundation set up by Ted Turner in support of the UN (see Chapter 15). Before joining the UN, Fréchette was the Deputy Minister of National Defence of Canada. She served as Permanent Representative of Canada to the UN from 1992–95.

international treaties and conventions. The problem comes when these rights seem to conflict with national boundaries. If mass murder is committed within a nation, does the world community have the obligation or the right to intervene to stop it? The usual response over the decades has been that international law does not cross national borders. And yet, the spirit of the UN Charter clearly should lead member states to act when human rights are being grossly violated.

Annan has proposed to alter the historical approach radically by arguing that international human rights law must apply in each member state, and that certain acts like genocide cannot be allowed to occur with impunity. He has based his view, no doubt, on his own bitter experience with events in places like Bosnia and Rwanda, where the UN was accused of doing too little to prevent mass murders. In 1995, during the dissolution of Yugoslavia, Serb militia in the Bosnian town of Srebrenica killed thousands of Muslim civilians in a so-called safe haven protected by UN peacekeepers. A report issued in late 1999 condemned the peacekeeping force for not acting to prevent the tragedy. The blame might better have fallen on the UN itself, and the Security Council specifically, for providing too few peacekeepers to constitute an effective defense; nevertheless, the peacekeeping effort had clearly failed. In Africa, during the 1994 civil war in Rwanda

Deputy Secretary General Louise
Fréchette, Mar. 5, 2002. UN/DPI
photo by Eskinder Debebe.

between Tutsi and Hutu tribes, hundreds of thousands of civilians
were murdered, sometimes in plain view of the international media.
Some of those killed included ten Belgian members of the UN Assistance Mission for Rwanda (UNAMIR), established in 1993 to monitor
a truce between the Hutu-dominated central government and Tutsi-led
insurgents based in neighboring Uganda. The UNAMIR commander,
General Romeo Dallaire of Canada, had warned about the possibility of
ethnic violence and asked for more forces, which the Security Council
finally authorized after the killing began, but member states were slow
to contribute contingents. The genocide continued until the Tutsi-led
insurgents reached the capital and installed a new government.

The Rwanda massacres occurred while Annan was UN Undersecretary General for Peacekeeping. After he became SG, Annan commissioned a report to examine what had happened and suggest remedies. When the report concluded that the sending of UN peacekeepers

could have prevented most of the deaths—an analysis by no means universally accepted, since the massacres occurred so quickly that effective UN response might have been difficult—Annan accepted responsibility for failing to act more quickly.

Annan formally stated his new approach to intervention in an address at the General Assembly in September 1999, in which he asked member states "to unite in the pursuit of more effective policies to stop organized mass murder and egregious violations of human rights." Conceding that there were many ways to intervene, he asserted that not only diplomacy but even armed action was an acceptable option. This provoked debate around the world. Rights organizations generally supported Annan's comments. Human Rights Watch hailed his statement as a "highlight" of 1999, a year when "sovereignty gave way in places where crimes against humanity were being committed." Others were less happy. They feared that the concept of "humanitarian intervention" might disguise unjustified interference in a nation's affairs, or might encourage secessionist movements to provoke gross violations of human rights in order to bring on an international presence that might aid their cause. There was concern that weak states were probably more likely than strong ones to suffer such intervention.

Acknowledging the value of arguments put forth by critics and skeptics, Annan has posed a difficult question: "If humanitarian intervention is, indeed, an unacceptable assault on sovereignty, how should we respond to a Rwanda, to a Srebrenica—to gross and systematic violations of human rights that offend every precept of our common humanity?" He has laid out the issues very clearly:

> We confront a real dilemma. Few would disagree that both the defense of humanity and the defense of sovereignty are principles that must be supported. Alas, that does not tell us which principle should prevail when they are in conflict. Humanitarian intervention is a sensitive issue, fraught with political difficulty and not susceptible to easy answers. But surely no legal principle—not even sovereignty—can ever shield crimes against humanity. Where such

crimes occur and peaceful attempts to halt them have been exhausted, the Security Council has a moral duty to act on behalf of the international community. The fact that we cannot protect people everywhere is no reason for doing nothing when we can. Armed intervention must always remain the option of last resort, but in the face of mass murder it is an option that cannot be relinquished.

No one has yet provided a generally accepted answer to Annan's question or been able to articulate a consistent alternative approach.

Although Annan's ideas about intervention are surely influenced by the UN's failures in places like Srebrenica, another factor is also involved. Annan has spoken often and vigorously about the need for the UN to imagine itself as an organization composed both of nations and of individuals. The Charter, he reminds listeners, delimits many individual rights and speaks not only of the world's nations but of its people. If the need to protect individual rights requires bypassing a national government, so be it. "Once and for all," he has said, "we must make clear that the rights for which we fight are not the rights of states or factions, but the rights of the individual human being to live in dignity and freedom."

Annan sees individual rights as central to the world of the future. In his view they are key elements in economic and social development. Abandoning the traditional view that modern nations progress through education and capital investments, followed by greater personal rights, he has reversed the order: human rights are a precondition for national development. Such "rights-based" development is gaining attention at the UN and elsewhere, as analysts ponder the inability of some nations to raise their social and economic levels despite years of development efforts and big loans and grants from the World Bank and other donor agencies. The logic is very powerful, but also very threatening to some governments that fear they will lose control over their citizens.

It is not yet clear whether Annan's new approach to rights and national sovereignty will prevail. But the fact that someone in his position has raised the issue suggests it is an idea whose time has

come. And it is significant that Annan's election to a second term as
SG came after, not before, he made his most controversial statements
on the subject.

A Cult of Personality?

It is hard to find anyone who can mount a serious criticism of Annan's performance as Secretary General. Mark Malloch Brown praises
his unusual combination of tact and firmness. "There are plenty of
people with tact that just give in to the lowest common denominator,"
he observes, and "plenty of people with firmness that fall at first
hurdle because they don't understand the need for cultural sensitivity." Annan, however, has both qualities and has used them to as-
semble "a genuine, multicultural management team, which is more
than a team, it's a force." In addition, says Malloch Brown, Annan has
made his office important internationally by being helpful to heads of
government and other leaders.

Secretary General Kofi Annan accepts the Nobel Peace Prize on Dec. 10,
2001, in Oslo, Norway. UN/DPI photo by Sergey Bermeniev.

Blame It on the Politicians

"An awful lot of us did graduate school in the US. . . . We feel comfortable with Americans because they are more multiculturally tolerant than other nationalities. The perverse thing is, the only one who doesn't like the UN is the American government. Washington is much more skeptical than the rest of America."
—Mark Malloch Brown, UNDP

So impressive has Annan been that the Security Council nominated him for a second term, ahead of schedule, and the General Assembly approved the choice by acclamation. He began his second and final term in 2001, the year he received the Nobel Peace Prize. He and US Secretary of State Colin Powell developed a close and strong working relationship—a rarity in UN–US relations during recent decades. He began to work amicably with the Bush administration, which was initially indifferent to the UN if not outright hostile.

The tough-minded Richard Holbrooke rates Annan "an astonishingly effective person considering the problems that he faces." Annan "combines a series of qualities that are inconceivable to find in one person: he's from Africa and has real stature in his native country; he is the first SG ever to know the bureaucracy from the inside; and he is married to a European who happens to be the niece of one of the great humanitarian figures [Raoul Wallenberg]. And he has great moral authority. You can't ever match that again."

If there is a downside to Annan's popularity, it comes from the very personal nature of his success. Malloch Brown argues that when Annan decides that something matters, like development or poverty reduction, the UN system and the world in general pay much more attention than if "the UN passes some dreary resolution." But Annan "doesn't seem to have coattails in terms of the UN system." Although he is esteemed by all, "even including Senator Helms, who considers Kofi his great friend," this admiration doesn't elevate the UN in general. "In that sense, Kofi has performed an extraordinary act of self-levitation. He hovers above the UN system, so to speak, in everybody's imagination, somehow personally not tainted by the shortcomings of the UN. But the corollary of that is that his extraordinary personal performance doesn't always seem to rub off in positive ways on the UN." The next Secretary General, Malloch Brown fears, will have to start from zero to build his or her credibility. A more charitable view might be that Annan's longest coattail is the cohort of smart and idealistic personnel he has appointed to important positions in the Secretariat.

Will Our Luck Hold?

Annan has a few years in which to strengthen his influence. The Secretary General is elected by the General Assembly for a renewable five-year term, and Annan will finish his tenure at the end of 2006. Possibly the main candidates are already drawing up their plans and preparing their campaign teams. The process of choosing the Secretary General involves two UN bodies: the Security Council, which recommends a candidate, and the General Assembly, which ratifies the choice. Candidates are unlikely to come from certain countries because they either raise too many animosities or complications, like

---

A Hostile Review

"I thought Kurt Waldheim was a terrible SG from the beginning. He didn't care about anything except his own political position. I remember the refugee conference in Geneva which he was supposed to chair, 1979, and how he went to Geneva but didn't appear. He said he had a sore throat. He wouldn't even come to sit quietly; he let someone else read his speech. People began to joke about it. We used to call him a Nazi, but we didn't realize he really was a Nazi."
—Richard Holbrooke

Secretary General Dag Hammarskjöld (left) and his successor, General Assembly President U Thant of Burma (right), listen to statements during the General Debate on Oct. 1, 1959. UN photo.

Libya, or are divided, like Korea. Political correctness often becomes an issue, because both the industrial and nonindustrial nations accept the notions, first, that no single nation or group of nations should dominate the world organization and, second, that the smaller and less developed countries should be guaranteed a strong voice.

For the past twenty years the unwritten agreement has been that the SG should rotate among regions of the world. Accordingly, Javier Perez de Cuellar, from South America, served two terms and was followed by Boutros Boutros-Ghali, from Africa, who served only one term. Kofi Annan succeeded him with the understanding that he would serve only one term. In fact, Annan will have served two terms, so Africa has contributed more than its "share" to the ranks of UN leaders. Because Europe has produced several Secretaries General, ending with Kurt Waldheim, the post ought to go next to Asia (which, in the UN system, includes the Arab states of the Middle East). But Asia is very big and diverse, so the number of potential donor countries would seem to be large. Not according to Richard Holbrooke, however. He points out that China is disqualified because the five permanent members of the Security Council are traditionally excluded from offering candidates. Japan is excluded, he argues, "because there is so much aversion to Japan and the Chinese won't want them." Holbrooke dismisses Korea because of the country's division between North and South, and asserts that India and Pakistan "cancel each other out." A candidate from an Arab state is not impossible but unlikely, he thinks. Among the other Asian nations, Holbrooke does not see an obvious choice. Burma provided one Secretary General, U Thant (1961–71), but then "disappeared into forty years of dictatorship." He discounts Indonesia's chances because of its recent political and social turmoil; Sri Lanka or Malaysia would be a stretch. "It's very limited," he concludes. "So your pool of countries is Philippines, Singapore, Thailand, Bangladesh. And that's probably it."

Or is it? The funny thing about election campaigns is that they don't always play out as the pollsters and pundits predict, as we know from our own national politics. It's hard to know what Asia will be like when it's time for the next Secretary General to be chosen, so even the most perceptive experts are making, at best, educated guesses.

CHAPTER 4

The American Ambassadors

But in the case of the American ambassador, there are multiple agencies within Washington involved. The State Department doesn't always have the last word. The President is sometimes in touch either directly or through the National Security Advisor. The Pentagon is never shy about being in touch. The American Ambassador at the UN has to sort through this and has to practice diplomacy with Washington even more than she or he practices diplomacy at the UN.
—David Malone, former Canadian diplomat and current
President of the International Peace Academy

Each member nation maintains a UN Mission in New York City, staffed by a head, known as the Permanent Representative, who also carries the title of Ambassador. The term of the Permanent Rep varies by nation, usually extending over several years. So the word "permanent" shouldn't be taken too literally, but it conveniently denotes the key person in a delegation of representatives. The current US Permanent Representative is John Negroponte, who succeeded Richard Holbrooke in 2001.

The US Permanent Rep has the highest-visibility job at the UN,

US Permanent Representatives to the UN, 1946–2002

Edward R. Stettinius Jr. (March 1946–June 1946)
Herschel V. Johnson (acting) (June 1946–January 1947)
Warren R. Austin (January 1947–January 1953)
Henry Cabot Lodge Jr. (January 1953–September 1960)
James J. Wadsworth (September 1960–January 1961)
Adlai E. Stevenson (January 1961–July 1965)
Arthur J. Goldberg (July 1965–June 1968)
George W. Ball (June 1968–September 1968)
James Russell Wiggins (October 1968–January 1969)
Charles W. Yost (January 1969–February 1971)
George H. W. Bush (February 1971–January 1973)
John P. Scali (February 1973–June 1975)
Daniel P. Moynihan (June 1975–February 1976)
William W. Scranton (March 1976–January 1977)
Andrew Young (January 1977–April 1979)
Donald McHenry (April 1979–January 1981)
Jeane J. Kirkpatrick (February 1981–April 1985)
Vernon A. Walters (May 1985–January 1989)
Thomas R. Pickering (March 1989–May 1992)
Edward J. Perkins (May 1992–January 1993)
Madeleine K. Albright (February 1993–January 1997)
Bill Richardson (February 1997–September 1998)
A. Peter Burleigh, Chargé d'Affaires (September 1998–August 1999)
Richard C. Holbrooke (August 1999–January 2001)
John Negroponte (September 2001–)

next to the Secretary General, and one of the most complicated owing
to US geopolitical eminence and the Byzantine nature of US policy-
making. "The job of an American ambassador at the UN is a particularly tough one," says David Malone. "Most ambassadors at the
UN get one set of instructions that are channeled through the foreign
minister and occasionally they will hear from their head of govern-

US Secretary of State Madeleine Albright and President of Mozambique
Joaquim Alberto Chissano meet before the Security Council's session on the
Congo on Jan. 24, 2000. UN/DPI photo by Eskinder Debebe.

ment or head of state. That's the case of France, for example, where
the head of state plays quite an active role." The US Ambassador,
however, has many bosses and many peers who feel free to make
suggestions and intervene in other ways. The greatest diplomatic skill
is required to manage such a complicated chain of command while
still being able to accomplish something at the UN.

Personal ambition adds another level of complexity. Malone suggests, for example, that when Madeleine Albright was Permanent Rep
she had "real influence" in Washington but preferred not to take risks
because she was angling for an even bigger job, which she got when
she became Secretary of State. She practiced "endless diplomacy,"
Malone claims, not so much in New York as in Washington, "in order
not to make enemies." In contrast, Richard Holbrooke felt sufficiently
strong in Washington to define a "Holbrooke policy" at the UN and
expect others to follow it. Amazingly, says Malone, they generally did.

Born in Prague, Madeleine Korbel Albright was the US Permanent Representative to the UN from 1993–97 and served as America's first female secretary of state from 1997–2001. Albright was a staff member on the National Security Council and at the White House, where she was responsible for foreign policy legislation, from 1978–81.

Richard C. Holbrooke was the US Permanent Representative to the UN from 1999–2001. While US Ambassador to Germany from 1993–94, and later Assistant Secretary of State for European and Canadian Affairs, he was also chief negotiator for the historic 1995 Dayton Peace Accords, which ended the war in Bosnia. Holbrooke began his career as a Foreign Service Officer in 1962, in Vietnam. He is vice chairman of Perseus, a private equity firm.

Bill Richardson was US Permanent Rep from 1997–1998, after having been a congressional representative from New Mexico. He left his UN position to become Secretary of the US Department of Energy, and is now governor of New Mexico.

"Nobody really spoke back to him. He had the ear of the President. The Vice President liked and respected him. . . . He essentially made policy on every subject that he discussed at the UN, and he then advised Washington on what their policy was henceforth to be. It was a very interesting performance."

The Current Head of Mission

With John Negroponte, the current Permanent Rep, Malone believes we have "returned to a career diplomat who is very skilled in dealing with other ambassadors of the UN. He telegraphs to them a respect

John D. Negroponte became US Permanent Representative to the UN on Sept. 18, 2001. As a member of the Career Foreign Service from 1960 to 1997, he served at posts in Asia and Europe, and was ambassador to Honduras and then Mexico. For several years he was executive vice president for global markets of The McGraw-Hill Companies.

for their country's position. He also telegraphs very consistent, conservative Washington views on what the UN should be doing."

Few Permanent Reps have assumed office under more difficult conditions. Negroponte was sworn in as United States Representative to the United Nations on September 18, 2001, only one week after 9/11, when the UN was consumed with trying to respond constructively in the emerging international alliance against terrorism. "I arrived here the 19th of September," he noted in a recent interview, "and my experience has been very much shaped by the events of September 11th and our response to that. The first several months were pretty much absorbed with the issue of terrorism and Afghanistan."

Negroponte's first months gave new meaning to the concept of on-the-job-training. Fortunately, he's a fast learner. His background as a career diplomat, with some experience at the White House, helped, along with his corporate experience dealing with global markets. He is very much a team player and a listener. "You've got to meet face to face with people to get yourself comfortable, to get comfortable with the policy issues," he has said.

Negroponte has found that while he needs all his diplomatic skills as US Permanent Rep, he uses them very differently. In some of his former diplomatic posts, such as ambassador to Mexico and to the Philippines, he had time to become an expert on each nation and culture, but at the UN he has to deal with an endless variety of people and issues. "To be a representative here, you have to know a little bit about a lot of issues. And managing your own time so you make sure you know what you need to know in order to be effective is a challenge because some days on your agenda there are three or four various conflicts that come up." He has likened the UN post to being a member of a legislature, and it has helped him understand what it's like to be a member of Congress. "You don't have complete control over your schedule, things come up all of a sudden. It's a bit like a three-ring circus. You've got the General Assembly, the Security Council, the six [General Assembly] committees. Things can come up in those committees that need your attention. I've noticed that I don't have as much control over my schedule or my agenda as I did when I was a bilateral ambassador."

Negroponte has also become familiar with the UN penchant for debates and resolutions, especially relating to Israel and the Palestinians. "I've been a little bit distressed by how much time does get absorbed on what I consider to be a pretty sterile Middle Eastern debate," he states. Conceding that some discussion about the Middle East has been constructive—particularly one resolution, 1397, that affirmed the vision of a Palestinian state, which the US Mission initiated—he nevertheless has been forced to conclude that "the protagonists see the UN as a forum, just another public arena, rather than a way of really devising solutions to problems." He is bothered by the "blame game" in which some delegations try to score points for short-term gain. That game wastes everyone's time and isn't very good for the UN, he believes, because it can undermine the UN's credibility.

To remedy the situation, Negroponte has been urging delegations to be patient once a resolution has been passed by the Security Council, rather than immediately calling for yet another resolution. "I think we've made some success," he has said, but it has been "the most exhausting part of my job."

Often, however, Negroponte finds that his hardest job is managing the home base. In New York City the UN has great public visibility and strong political support. "There is a natural constituency," says Negroponte. "But outside of NY and outside the beltway, that's more of a challenge."

CHAPTER 5

The Security Council

Article 24
In order to ensure prompt and effective action by the United Nations,
its Members confer on the Security Council primary responsibility for
the maintenance of international peace and security, and agree that in
carrying out its duties under this responsibility the Security Council acts on
their behalf. —UN Charter

The Security Council is the UN's enforcer, charged with making the world a safer, more stable place by preventing or stopping armed conflict among and even within nations. The council has the authority to examine any conflict or dispute that might have international repercussions. It can identify aggressive action by states and call on UN members to make an appropriate response, including application of economic sanctions and even military action. Consequently, the council must be ready to deliberate at any time.

The SC is the only UN body whose resolutions are legally binding. It has the authority to decide matters affecting the fate of governments, establish peacekeeping missions, create tribunals to try persons accused of war crimes, and in extreme cases declare a nation to

From the UN Charter

ARTICLE 41

The Security Council may decide what measures not involving the use of armed force are to be employed to give effect to its decisions, and it may call upon the Members of the United Nations to apply such measures. These may include complete or partial interruption of economic relations and of rail, sea, air, postal, telegraphic, radio and other means of communication, and the severance of diplomatic relations.

ARTICLE 42

Should the Security Council consider that measures provided for in Article 41 would be adequate or have proved to be inadequate, it may take such action by air, sea, or land forces as may be necessary to maintain or restore international peace and security. Such action may include demonstrations, blockades, and other operations by air, sea, or land forces of Members of the United Nations.

be fair game for corrective action by other member states. Richard Holbrooke has called the Security Council "the most important international body in the world. Countries give it a legitimacy because it can authorize the use of force for peacemaking or even a war, as in Korea, Kuwait, and Afghanistan."

Big Job, Big Tools

The council has tools to match this very big job. It has fifteen members, ten of them elected by the General Assembly to two-year terms. The other five—the Permanent 5, or P5, which have veto power over resolutions—are China, France, the Russian Federation, the United

Security Council Composition

Permanent Five (P5) members: China, France, Russia, UK, and US
Nonpermanent members: 3 Africans, 2 Latin Americans, 1 Arab, 1
Asian, 1 Eastern European, and 2 Western Europeans

Kingdom, and the United States. Acting as a sort of club, the permanent members usually play a leading role in deliberations. The council is presided over by the president, an office that rotates monthly,
according to the English alphabetical listing of SC member states.

It takes nine votes to pass a resolution. A permanent member can
abstain from voting if it does not want to take a public stand on the
measure. However, if it objects to the measure but cannot find the
votes to defeat it, it can exercise a veto as a last resort. Each member of the P5 has used the veto. Vetoes were more common during
the cold war, when the world was divided into Communist and non-
Communist blocs, but in recent years they have become rare (see
Table 1). The most recent veto was by the US, on December 20, 2002,
against a Syrian resolution that condemned Israel for destroying a UN
facility on the West Bank and killing several staff.

Following the US Star

According to David Malone, "in the Security Council the US is very
much the dominant power. Nothing can be done against its wishes. Its
active support is required for major decisions. It is also prepared to
accommodate other countries every now and then, but it's more used
to being accommodated itself." The United States has become deeply
engaged in the SC when it has seen advantages for its own international interests and policies. As Madeleine Albright has commented,
the UN's ability to intervene in certain emergencies often reduces the
job of the United States: "This serves our interest because when the US

The Security Council holds its first summit-level meeting on Jan. 31, 1992.
UN/DPI photo by M. Grant.

intervenes alone, we pay all of the costs and run all of the risks. When
the UN acts, we pay a quarter of the costs and others provide the vast
majority of troops."

The United Kingdom and France also play leading roles in the
council. Malone says they "work much harder than any of the other
permanent members to come up with initiatives in areas far and wide.
They send people of extraordinary skill to the council. If one looks at
the current ambassadors of Britain and France they are both superb
operators with good staffs. They have hit the ground running faster
than anyone else. The British are notorious for always having a draft

An Important Distinction

"You have to make a distinction between the UN as an institution and an organization, on the one hand, and the member states, particularly the Permanent 5, on the other. It's axiomatic that the solid achievements of the Security Council have tended to be when the P5 can act in harmony or consensus. If there is either strong disagreement or reluctance on the part of one or more of the P5 members, that's when you start getting into difficulties."
—John Negroponte, US Ambassador to the UN

in their back pocket. For these countries, their permanent membership really matters to their international identity precisely because their role in the world has shrunk. They're working very hard to stay permanent members of the Security Council."

The larger countries are usually more active on the council than the smaller ones because they have the staff time needed to keep up with the constantly increasing load. Recalls Richard Holbrooke, "Tom Pickering told me that when he was ambassador, the Security Council met two or three times a month. Now it meets almost every day. It's a nonstop forum for discussion, much of it useless."

Table 1 shows that the number of annual meetings has tripled since 1988, from 55 to 167, while the number of resolutions adopted has risen two and a half times, from 20 to 50.

The Need for Leadership

Although the council has a small membership compared with the General Assembly, and tries to operate by consensus, it works most efficiently and effectively when one of the P5 exercises leadership. Absent decisive guidance, it may dither and flounder, as it often did with Iraq during the late 1990s. The Iraq case shows not only the

Table 1 Security Council Meetings, Resolutions, and Vetoes, 1988–2000

Year	Meetings	Resolutions Considered	Resolutions Adopted	US Vetoes
2000	167	52	50	0
1999	124	67	65	0
1998	116	73	73	0
1997	117	57	54	2
1996	114	59	57	1
1995	130	67	66	1
1994	160	78	77	0
1993	171	95	93	0
1992	129	74	74	0
1991	53	42	42	0
1990	69	40	37	2
1989	69	25	20	5
1988	55	26	20	6

Source: Adapted from US Department of State, *18th Annual Report on Voting Practices in the UN, 2000*, p. 86.

importance of leadership but the need to have a consensus view of what constitutes leadership. When Iraq invaded Kuwait in 1990, the Security Council acted quickly to condemn the invasion and impose sanctions to encourage the world community to expel the attacker. The US took the leading role in acting as champion of the Kuwaiti people and representative of the world community in the UN forum. The US-led coalition defeated the Iraqi forces in 1991 and liberated Kuwait; however, the council's resolve began to drain away as the urgency of war became a memory and the battered Iraqi military seemed to pose little threat to neighboring countries.

The council's main concerns about Iraq after the war centered on the issue of disarmament. The cease-fire agreement ending the war stipulated that Iraq would surrender or destroy all its so-called weapons of mass destruction, meaning biological, chemical, and nuclear weapons. During the Gulf War the Iraqis shot off scores of SCUD missiles that were inaccurate but had considerable psychological impact on civilians. They would have been far more terrifying if they had carried chemical or nuclear warheads—not an outlandish notion considering the strong interest of the Saddam Hussein regime in acquiring such technology. The UN gained the right, under the cease-fire, to send inspectors to examine arms facilities to ensure Iraq's compliance. The job of finding any such weapons fell to the United Nations Special Commission (UNSCOM), assisted by the International Atomic Energy Agency (IAEA). During the next seven years, despite both passive and active resistance from Saddam's regime, UNSCOM supervised the destruction of thousands of weapons and chemical munitions.

When UNSCOM pulled out its inspectors in 1998, Saddam's regime banned their return, which prevented the UN from giving Iraq a clean bill of health and lifting sanctions. None of the members of the P5 took a strong enough stand to force Saddam's regime to comply with the terms of the cease-fire and admit inspectors. The best the Security Council could do was to replace UNSCOM in 1999 with a new entity, the UN Monitoring, Verification, and Inspection Commission (UNMOVIC), in the hope of making a fresh start and finally getting proof that Iraq no longer possessed weapons of mass destruction. The Security Council was divided about how to handle Saddam, until pressure from the US government brought clarity to the situation. At the General Assembly in September 2002, President Bush challenged the UN to enforce its own resolutions concerning Iraq. In November, the P5 hammered out a resolution that gave Iraq a final opportunity to disarm fully. Saddam, faced with a resolute Security Council and a very threatening United States, began slowly and grudgingly to comply during the early months of 2003. In the US view, the belated Iraqi response was inadequate and more apparent than real, while some Security Council members took the opposite view and declared that Iraq was finally responding forthrightly to the council's demands. In March the US and Great Britain invaded Iraq, despite the objections of the other members of the P5. When the brief war ended, efforts were made in the council and the General Assembly to condemn the invasion, but they failed. US Permanent Rep John Negroponte attributes the failure partly to the intense discussion among SC members, during which "countries became familiar enough with our position and had enough of their own discussion that the proponents of condemning us in the council and in the General Assembly were unable to muster sufficient votes to get that done. Or, at least countries gave the matter sufficient thought to conclude that whatever reservations they might have, it wasn't worth it for them politically, they didn't want to incur the political cost or the political friction of further disagreeing with the United States on this issue."

Other Ways of Thinking about Security

The Security Council has traditionally viewed security as an issue of physical assault. The Universal Declaration of Human Rights, however, lists an array of securities, such as freedom from hunger, the right to adequate housing and decent employment, and the right to live in a healthy environment (see Appendix B). Does the Security Council also oversee these forms of security? Historically the answer has been no. Rather, the council has left these matters to other parts of the UN system, especially the various agencies, programs, and commissions established to address issues like food supply, disaster relief, and health care. This has its logic, because the SC imagines itself as an executive body more than an administrative system. Recently, however, the council did formally address a health-related issue on the grounds that vital security interests were at stake. US Ambassador Richard Holbrooke set precedent by persuading the Security Council to discuss the impact of the AIDS crisis in Africa in January 2000 at a meeting chaired by US Vice President Al Gore. A State Department report noted that while the discussion was "controversial at the time," it set the stage for a later council meeting and resolution about AIDS and caused language about HIV/AIDS to be included in peacekeeping resolutions.

Reforming the Council

In recent years, many UN member states have begun urging a change of the Security Council to make it more reflective of today's international realities. Since the council was created in 1945, more than a hundred nations have come into existence, and former pariah states like Japan, Germany, and South Africa have rejoined the world community, while many developing nations have become economic and trade dynamos. Yet the council still operates on the same basic principles and with the same P5. Formal debates about reform have occurred in the General Assembly, and informal discussions occur everywhere in the UN system as participants advance their particular agendas and seek allies. "Reform" is always a loaded word because its meaning is often so subjective and because any significant change will affect power relationships and the status of particular member states.

One suggested change is to expand the number of council members. The Japanese, who would like to gain a permanent seat, have suggested raising the number from fifteen to twenty-four members and possibly restricting the veto. The current arrangement gives the P5 the right to veto any resolution and to exercise the veto as often as they like. If the veto power is curbed, that might profoundly change the ways in which the P5 view the council, because they would no longer be assured of protecting their own interests. Kofi Annan has gone on record supporting additional permanent seats and increasing the core group to a P7 or P8. This might be less threatening to the P5 because it slightly waters down their individual impact without diminishing the ability to cast the veto. It would, however, complicate relations among veto holders by increasing the number of parties who need to be engaged in the kind of consensus-building that gives the P5 so much power in the UN.

Some insiders wonder if the reform advocates fully understand the impact of their proposed changes. "Any expansion risks making the council unworkable because it would become so big," claims Nancy Soderberg. "If you expand it you will just have more side groups to

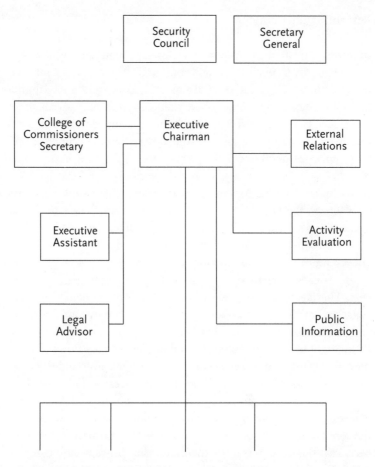

Organizational chart of the UN Monitoring, Verification, and Inspection Commission (UNMOVIC). This commission was created by Security Council resolution 1284 of December 17, 1999, with the task of disarming Iraq of weapons of mass destruction. Hans Blix of Sweden was the commission's Executive Chairman until 2003. BW = biological weapons; CW = chemical weapons; M = missiles.

Administrative Service	Division of Technical Support and Training	Division of Planning and Operations	Division of Analysis and Assessment	Division of Information
Budget and Finance	Equipment, analytical services, procurement	Baghdad BW Ongoing Monitoring and CW Verification Center	BW	Export/import joint unit
Personnel, recruitment, health and safety	Communications, transportation, security		CW	Imagery
			M	Outside information sources
Translation and interpretation	Training	Multidisciplinary inspections (including export/import and IAEA)	Multidisciplinary inspections (analysis)	
	Bahrain field office			Data Processing and archives

Team Players at Last

"If something really matters to the US, Britain, or France, or indeed to some of the nonpermanent members of the council, Russia rarely stands in the way. China never stands in the way. China and Russia don't play the wrecker role that they used to during the cold war. The Russians and Chinese have become genuinely post–cold war players in the Security Council."   —David Malone

work out things. You can't have an efficient body and negotiate with 26 people on it." She agrees that the Europeans shouldn't have so many seats, especially with the European Union: "How can you argue for four European countries on the council when Africa and Asia get one? It's just not going to fly. . . . You're not going to have meaningful council expansion until you have a rotating EU seat with a veto." She plausibly argues that such changes won't happen soon, because the member states that must agree on it "are not going to put themselves out of power, nor will the US work to get rid of its two best allies, France and the UK, in the council."

To members like France, Great Britain, and the United States, which have enjoyed a preeminent role in the council, calls for change may seem like gratuitous tinkering—but they cannot be ignored. Recently, the US suggested it could support an expanded council including consideration of three new permanent seats for representatives from the developing countries of Asia, Africa, and Latin America and the Caribbean. The US wanted no change in the status or privileges of the existing permanent members as outlined in the UN Charter, including any limitations on the veto. Even if the US were to embrace reform of the council enthusiastically, reform might still not happen soon owing to the sharp differences of opinion among member states about which of them should be admitted to an enlarged council. Members of major regional groupings, such as Africa or Asia, have been unable to agree on which of them should be selected for a permanent council seat.

The locus for formal discussion is in the General Assembly, in a committee with the catchy name of the Open-Ended Working Group on the Question of Equitable Representation on and Increase in the Membership of the Security Council (OEWG). It has met for nearly a decade without being able to reach a consensus on a "framework resolution" for consideration by the full assembly, so the process of Security Council reform remains ongoing.

CHAPTER 6

Peace Operations

Article 43
All Members of the United Nations, in order to contribute to the mainte-
nance of international peace and security, undertake to make available to
the Security Council, on its call and in accordance with a special agreement
or agreements, armed forces, assistance, and facilities, including rights of
passage, necessary for the purpose of maintaining international peace and
security. —UN Charter

Although peacekeeping is one of the quintessential UN functions, it is mentioned only briefly in the Charter. Its full scope and nature have gradually emerged, through need, as a middle ground between mere arbitration of disputes, on the one hand, and use of armed force, on the other. The Security Council's first peacekeeping resolution set important precedents, establishing the United Nations Truce Super-vision Organization (UNTSO) in 1948 to oversee the truce between Arabs and Jews when the United Kingdom left Palestine. Like peace-keepers today, the UNTSO troops were provided by member states. The troopers wore the blue helmets that have marked UN peace-keepers ever since. UNTSO also set the model for nomenclature: it is invariably referred to by its acronym rather than its full name. That decades-old practice has led to a roster of past and current operations that read like a chapter out of Genesis, with names that sound like the biblical Gog and Magog—actually, MOONUC and UNOMIG. UNTSO is still in operation, with an expanded mandate that includes supervising the implementation and observance of the general agreements between Israel and its four Arab neighbors.

Once the Security Council authorizes the deployment of an operation, defines its mission, and recommends how it should be carried out, the Secretary General appoints a Force Commander and through the Secretariat's Department of Peacekeeping Operations (DPKO) arranges for management and logistics. Member states are asked to provide personnel, equipment, and logistics. The UN pays member states at the rate of $1,100 per peacekeeper per month, and the governments pay the troops according to their own scales. Member states retain control over their units. Peacekeeping personnel rely less on their arms than on their international authority and their reputation for impartiality. They wear their country's uniform and are identified as peacekeepers by a UN blue helmet or a beret and a badge.

Some UN peacekeeping operations consist of military observers charged with monitoring truces, troop withdrawals, and borders or demilitarized zones. Other operations involve military formations capable of acting as buffers between hostile forces. More recently, some peacekeeping operations have combined military and police or civilian functions and personnel, with the aim of creating or strengthening political institutions, providing emergency aid, clearing land mines, or administering and monitoring free elections.

Peace-related issues have always been central to Security Council deliberations, but in the past decade they have become especially numerous and demanding of time and resources. The decade of the 1990s saw the UN launch more peace-related operations than in all the previous four decades. During the year ending June 2003 there were 14 peacekeeping missions, employing 45,000 personnel at a cost of $2.6 billion.

And the nature of the disputes has largely changed. The norm used

A Peace Glossary

Just as Eskimos have many words to describe the various kinds of snow, the UN has developed words and phrases for the making and keeping of peace. Here are just a few.

preventive diplomacy
As its name suggests, preventive diplomacy seeks to head off disputes before they become full-blown conflicts. The UN prefers this kind of diplomacy but is able to apply it in only some instances. The UN employs its extensive contacts and offices around the world to detect early signs of potential threats to international peace and security.

peacemaking
Peacemaking involves the use of diplomacy to persuade belligerents to stop fighting and negotiate an end to their dispute.

peace enforcement
Peace enforcement involves the use of force against one of the belligerents to enforce an end to the fighting.

peace-building
Peace-building involves helping nations promote peace before, during, or after a conflict. Broadly defined, it employs a wide range of political, humanitarian, and human rights activities and programs.

to be that wars occurred between nation-states, which fought with field armies that were supposed to target combatants and not civilians—that was the theory, anyway. But these days nation-states have been remarkably well behaved toward one another, and in some places, like Europe, they have even forged close political ties. Instead, conflicts tend to occur within nations, in the form of civil wars (as in Rwanda, Congo, and the former Yugoslavia) or national resistance

Many parts of the UN system may join in a peace-building effort, as well as private bodies like nongovernmental organizations (NGOs). The Secretary General often appoints representatives to coordinate the activities through special peace-building support offices, such as those established in Liberia, Guinea-Bissau, and the Central African Republic.

the responsibility to protect
The Charter gives the UN the right to intervene in a nation's affairs to prevent egregious human rights violations, but in recent years there has been talk about a variant on this, called the responsibility to protect. A recent international commission stated in its report that "the responsibility to protect implies an evaluation of the issues from the point of view of those seeking or needing support, rather than those who may be considering intervention."

movements (like the East Timorese against Indonesian occupation, the Islamic separatists in the Philippines, the independence fighters in Kosovo, or the Palestinians against the Israelis).

The Talking Cure

Today, the council has to address so many requests for making or keeping peace that it usually begins by looking for a solution that does not involve a UN deployment. It starts with behind-the-scenes diplomacy, escalating to open diplomacy as needed.

A good example is the conflict between Ethiopia and its breakaway province of Eritrea, which began in the 1990s and has only recently been resolved, largely through UN and regional efforts. During the early 1980s, Ethiopia, a landlocked country, unilaterally annexed Eritrea, which gave it a port on the Red Sea; but the Eritreans resisted and finally secured their independence after a long war. Then, on May 6,

1998, the Eritrean government ordered its armed forces to occupy a slice of disputed territory on the border with Ethiopia. A regional body, the Organization of African Unity (OAU), worked out an agreement for settling the dispute, but neither side would commit to it.

In February 1999, the Security Council stepped in and urged the disputants to accept the OAU's plan. When they refused and began fighting, the council moved to its next stage of action, which was to tell the combatants to stop fighting, start talking, and arrange a cease-fire. The US also joined the cease-fire efforts, and in February and March OAU special envoy Ahmed Ouyahia (of Algeria) and former US National Security Advisor Anthony Lake visited Asmara and Addis Ababa. Algeria then brought the two parties together for talks, which broke down.

The fighting had by then stopped but seemed on the verge of resuming when, in April, the council reiterated its demand for a cease-fire and implementation of the OAU's plan. In June, the council again asked the two parties to negotiate, citing a looming humanitarian crisis as drought and unrest threatened massive starvation. The US sent more than 700,000 metric tons of food assistance to Ethiopia and 100,000 to Eritrea. A UN Security Council mission to Congo, led by US Permanent Representative Richard Holbrooke, began shuttle diplomacy during several days early in May, with Holbrooke leaning on both sides not to renew the fighting.

The shuttle talks failed, the mission left, and on May 12, 2000, Ethiopia sent its forces deep into Eritrea. The Security Council passed a resolution demanding an end to military action, but the next day Ethiopia's forces made a major breakthrough and eventually advanced to within a hundred kilometers of the Eritrean capital. Then the Ethiopian government, apparently satisfied it had acquired a good bargaining position, stated it was ending the war. Meanwhile, the Security Council passed another resolution, 1298, requiring that member states enforce an arms sales embargo on both combatants. Eritrea then declared that it would move its troops back to the border that existed in May 1998.

As each combatant backed off, the OAU, UN, and other parties arranged for new talks in Algiers, which led to an agreement on June 18 for a cease-fire. Once the fighting ended, the council created the UN Mission in Ethiopia and Eritrea (UNMEE), charged with monitoring the border and ensuring that the provisions of the cease-fire were honored. The council authorized the mission at a strength of more than 4,200 military and other personnel.

By then, Ethiopia and Eritrea had been fighting or at least glaring at each other for more than two years. Why did the council wait so long? The answer is that UN peacekeepers maintain peace once it is agreed to by the combatants, but they do not create peace through military action. The main purpose of peacekeeping is simply to help prevent fighting from erupting and to give negotiators a chance to find a permanent resolution to the dispute.

A resolution seems to have been found in the Ethiopia–Eritrea border dispute. In fall 2000, the OAU envoy and Anthony Lake pursued shuttle diplomacy while members of the Security Council urged the disputants to negotiate a complete solution. At Algiers in December 2000 the two nations signed a final accord in the presence of Secretary General Kofi Annan and US Secretary of State Madeleine Albright. The end is in sight but not quite achieved. UNMEE is expected to remain deployed until the final border between the two nations is demarcated, and until the two governments establish sufficient dialogue to ensure that they can peacefully resolve any disagreements or misunderstandings that might arise between them.

UN Sanctions

Sanctions are nonlethal, noninvasive mechanisms aimed at preventing a state from interacting with the outside world in certain ways, such as engaging in trade or acquiring arms. Travel bans and financial or diplomatic restrictions are also types of sanction. Although sanctions are intended to pressure governments, they may also unintentionally harm civilians too. Sometimes it is the poorest or most vulnerable

Fourteen countries had been subject to UN sanctions as of June 2003:

Afghanistan	Rwanda
Angola (lifted)	Sierra Leone
Ethiopia and Eritrea (lifted)	Somalia
Haiti (lifted)	South Africa (lifted)
Iraq (mostly lifted)	Southern Rhodesia (lifted)
Liberia	Sudan (lifted)
Libya (suspended)	The former Yugoslavia (lifted)

members of society who are most harmed when their nation is placed under a sanction, especially one that affects trade and commerce. Consider the case of Saddam Hussein's regime in Iraq, after the Gulf War.

When Iraq invaded Kuwait in 1990, the UN imposed sweeping sanctions intended to bar the aggressor from all trade and financial dealings, except for humanitarian purposes, with the rest of the world. After the US and its allies, with the blessing of the UN, routed the Iraqi armed forces and arranged a cease-fire (which the UN monitored) in 1991, the UN left the sanctions in place while stipulating that Iraq divest itself of weapons of mass destruction. Because the Iraqi government was not fully cooperating with inspections, the UN continued the sanctions throughout the years of the Saddam Hussein regime.

The Iraqi government, meanwhile, was able to partly evade the sanctions while complaining noisily that its citizens were being deprived of access to vital medicines, food, and other necessities. This effective campaign influenced the Security Council to create the Oil for Food program, which permitted the Iraqi government the option of exporting specified amounts of crude oil, under UN scrutiny, in order to pay for "humanitarian goods." Terms of the program were liberalized in 1998 and 1999, and finally in 2002, to give Iraq access to most civilian goods. The last liberalization was done through a Security Council resolution offered by the US in May 2002. The idea behind the resolution was to replace typical UN sanctions with "smart sanctions" that would enable Iraqi citizens to get necessities more easily while making it more difficult for Saddam Hussein's regime to use trade in order to obtain arms and other forbidden items. On May 22, 2003, two months after the US-led invasion of Iraq, the Security Council lifted sanctions, except for the sale of weapons and related materiel.

Rethinking Peacekeeping

Although traditional peacekeeping remains important, it is increasingly regarded as merely the first step in a process of moving from armed conflict to political dialogue and engagement. The new approach tries to engage all stakeholders in dialogue, which means governments, of course, but also nongovernmental organizations (which represent civil society and will be discussed in Chapter 18) and other groups. Among the pioneers of the new approach is Kofi Annan, who spent four years in charge of peacekeeping operations when he was Undersecretary General, and one of his top aides, Shashi Tharoor. As Tharoor says of his experiences during the 1990s, when the new approach emerged, in addition to doing the usual peacekeeping tasks they were experimenting with "all sorts of new things, everything from delivering humanitarian aid under fire, hunting down warlords, and of course monitoring no-fly zones. It was very much like fixing the engine of a moving car."

One of the places where the UN has applied its new thinking about peacekeeping is East Timor, which recently gained national independence from Indonesia. The Security Council hosted the negotiations that led in 1999 to a popular referendum in which the Timorese rejected autonomy within Indonesia and opted for complete independence. But the council had to authorize a multinational security force after Indonesian-backed militants unleashed a campaign of system-

East Timor independence leader Xanana Gusmao greets Secretary General Kofi Annan during his trip to East Timor in February 2000. UN/DPI photo by Eskinder Debebe.

atic destruction and violence in response to the Timorese referendum. Many East Timorese were killed and more than 200,000 were forced to flee, most of them to West Timor.

In October 1999, acting under Chapter VII of the UN Charter, the Security Council established the UN Transitional Administration in East Timor (UNTAET) to restore order and provide administrative services as East Timor prepared for independence. The SC appointed Sergio Vieira de Mello of Brazil as the Transitional Administrator for East Timor. UNTAET began a program of "Timorization" of key government posts to prepare for transition to full independence. In July UNTAET established the East Timor Transitional Administration (ETTA), with a cabinet of nine ministries, five headed by East Timorese. Then UNTAET appointed a thirty-six-member National Council representing a wide spectrum of Timorese society. UNTAET began preparations for elections in late summer 2001 for a national assembly, which drew up and adopted a constitution. In 2002 the Timorese elected a president and became a new nation.

The UN's nation-building has succeeded in launching East Timor on its new path, but interestingly the effort has gotten mixed reviews. David Malone praises its director: "To make good things happen at the UN requires particular skills and qualities that may not be required in running a major corporation or running a major government. They are particular skills of endurance and determination that I think find expression in Sergio Vieira de Mello, who pulled off the East Timor operation in spite of tremendous problems on the ground and enormous bureaucratic inertia within the UN. He just has the sheer determination to get things done and they did get done." Shepard Forman concedes that the effort went fairly well but questions whether it was appropriate: "The UN as a government in Kosovo and East Timor is questionable. Few of the people that went out to govern had any more experience than any of the East Timorese. That's an example of where it [the UN] took on a role to prove itself, and it did an all right job, but we lost a year or so in terms of the Timoreses' own capacity to develop, to reconstruct."

Good, bad, or inappropriate, the UN's mission to East Timor shows that new ideas are floating about and being acted on, which is crucial if the world body is going to adapt and remain vital. Which opens up another area of change: the faces under those blue helmets.

New Peacekeepers, New Faces

A relic of the colonial era, which didn't end until the 1970s, is that the Western media tend to present the European-American nations as militarily superior. This is increasingly an outdated notion. David Malone says, "It's just assumed that the West, because it is so well equipped when it goes into the peacekeeping field, is the only region providing qualified peacekeepers." Not so, he asserts. The Indians and the Pakistanis are "excellent peacekeepers," and the Bangladeshis and the Kenyans "have proved very good in the field." As proof he cites the case of the UN peacekeeping mission established in Rwanda in 1993, the same mission that was unable to stop the genocide between Hutus and Tutsis. The commander, Canadian general Romeo Dallaire, led a mixed force of Europeans and Ghanaians, who were outnumbered by the killers and suffered casualties as they tried to protect specific groups of victims. The Ghanaian peacekeepers saved the most lives, according to Malone, under their own brigadier general, Dallaire's deputy. "About 500 of them stayed behind and they saved at least 25,000 lives in the Kigali stadium and elsewhere," he says. "They never received any attention at all, and this tells us something about the way that peacekeeping is covered by the media. Dallaire has constantly tried to draw attention to the heroic behavior of the Ghanaians, but never with any success whatsoever."

Malone's own solution is to combine the technical prowess of the West with the commitment and courage of the Africans and other peacekeepers. "What is important in peacekeeping is that some of the Western militaries have the high-tech capacities that, say, the Ghanaian army doesn't have. So ideally a peacekeeping force in Africa will be composed of a mix of developing-country contingents and Western contingents."

Equally needed, as Malone and other insiders would agree, is a basic overhaul of how the UN constitutes and funds its peacekeeping missions. Imagine having to conduct potentially risky and difficult military operations when you don't have a standing army and lack the right to levy taxes. Understandably, the attempt to enlarge the peacekeeping concept along lines described above has stretched the peacekeeping effort sometimes beyond what it can handle. Some have likened UN peacekeeping to a volunteer fire department—but it's not that well organized, according to Kofi Annan, because for every mission it is necessary to scrounge up the fire engines and the money to pay for them "before we can start dousing any flames."

The Security Council commissioned a study led by Lakhdar Brahimi, the former Foreign Minister of Algeria, to examine the main shortcomings of the current operation and offer solutions for change. This so-called Brahimi report, submitted in August 2000, has become

The Size and Cost of Peacekeeping

Current Operations, as of June 2003

personnel

Military personnel and civilian police serving in missions on May 31, 2003   34,941

Countries contributing military personnel and civilian police on May 31, 2003   89

International civilian personnel on May 31, 2003   3,215

Local civilian personnel on May 31, 2003   6,665

Total number of fatalities in peacekeeping operations since 1948 as of May 31, 2003   1,797

financial aspects

Approved budgets for the period from July 1, 2002–June 30, 2003 About $2.63 billion

Estimated total cost of operations from 1948 to June 30, 2003 About $28.73 billion

Outstanding contributions to peacekeeping on May 31, 2003   About $1.15 billion

Note: The term "military personnel" refers to military observers and troops, as applicable. Fatality figures include military, civilian police, and civilian international and local personnel. Prepared by the United Nations Department of Public Information, Peace, and Security Section, in consultation with the Department of Peacekeeping Operations and the Peacekeeping Financing Division, Office of Program Planning, Budget and Accounts.

untso since june 1948
UN Truce Supervision Organization
Strength: military 154; international civilian 102; local civilian 113
Fatalities: 38
Appropriation for year 2003: $25.9 million

unmogip since january 1949
UN Military Observer Group in India and Pakistan
Strength: military 45; int'l civilian 24; local civilian 47
Fatalities: 9
Appropriation for year 2003: $9.2 million

unficyp since march 1964
UN Peacekeeping Force in Cyprus
Strength: military 1,248; civilian police 35; int'l civilian 44; local civilian 105
Fatalities: 170
Approved budget 07/03–06/04: $45.77 million (gross)
including voluntary contributions of $14.57 million from Cyprus and $6.5 million from Greece

undof since june 1974
UN Disengagement Observer Force
Strength: military 1,043; int'l civilian 37; local civilian 87
Fatalities: 40
Approved budget 07/03–06/04: $41.81 million (gross)

unifil since march 1978
UN Interim Force in Lebanon
Strength: military 2,029; int'l civilian 114; local civilian 302
Fatalities: 246
Approved budget 07/03–06/04: $94.06 million (gross)

unikom since april 1991
UN Iraq-Kuwait Observation Mission
Strength: military 13; int'l civilian 56; local civilian 162
Fatalities: 17
Commitment authority 07/03–10/03: $12 million

minurso since april 1991
UN Mission for the Referendum in Western Sahara
Strength: military 229; civilian police 25; int'l civilian 167; local civilian
120
Fatalities: 10
Approved budget 07/03–06/04: $43.4 million (gross)

unomig since august 1993
UN Observer Mission in Georgia
Strength: military 116; int'l civilian 99; local civilian 176
Fatalities: 7
Approved budget 07/03–06/04: $32.10 million (gross)

unmik since june 1999
UN Interim Administration Mission in Kosovo
Strength: civilian police 4,097; military 38; int'l civilian 1,005; local
civilian 3,184
Fatalities: 22
Approved budget 07/03–06/04: $329.74 million (gross)

unamsil since october 1999
UN Mission in Sierra Leone
Strength: military 13,804; civilian police 119; int'l civilian 310; local
civilian 577
Fatalities: 109
Approved budget 07/03–06/04: $543.49 million (gross)

monuc since december 1999
UN Organization Mission in the Democratic Republic of the Congo
Strength: military 4,515; civilian police 60; int'l civilian 603; local
civilian 708
Fatalities: 17
Approved budget 07/03–06/04: $608.23 million (gross)

unmee since july 2000
UN Mission in Ethiopia and Eritrea
Strength: military 4,077; int'l civilian 236; local civilian 260
Fatalities: 3
Approved budget 07/03–06/04: $196.89 million (gross)

unmiset since may 20, 2002
UN Mission of Support in East Timor
Strength: military 3,497; civilian police 517; int'l civilian 418; local civilian 824
Fatalities: 11
Approved budget 07/03–06/04: $193.34 million (gross)

minuci since may 2003
UN Mission in Côte d'Ivoire
Maximum authorized strength: 26 military liaison officers in the initial period and up to 50 additional officers as needed, and a small civilian staff
Estimated financial implications for a one-year period: $26.9 million (gross)
Adapted from "United Nations Peacekeeping Operations,"
http: //www.un.org/Depts/dpko/home.shtml

a blueprint for such efforts. The report recommends that the UN make fundamental changes in its policies and practices of peacekeeping and that it provide more financial backing. It urges an updating of the concept of peacekeeping to address modern situations where the combatants may be heavily armed and not always obedient to commanders or political leaders. In such highly charged scenarios the peacekeepers may have to choose sides, at least temporarily, in order to protect the innocent. The Security Council must therefore provide peacekeeping missions with precise instructions on how to act in a variety of possible circumstances. Equally important, according to the report, is the integration of military functions with historically civil concerns such as human rights, policing, and food, shelter, and medical services. The UN has begun acting on the report, beginning with the Security Council's acceptance of the report's recommendations. Questions now are whether the General Assembly will deliver adequate financial support and whether the council and the Secretariat have the will to follow through on the report over the long term.

CHAPTER 7

The General Assembly

Article 9
1. The General Assembly shall consist of all the Members of the United
Nations
2. Each Member shall have not more than five representatives in the Gen-
eral Assembly   —UN Charter

The General Assembly is both more and less than it seems to be.
Although modeled on national parliaments, it has a global purview
and visibility that no national legislature can match. It is a center
for discussion and debate among all the world's governments. Every
member state, no matter how big or small, has a seat and one vote.
The GA starts its official year with opening sessions, usually on the
third Tuesday of each September. A week later, at the General Debate,
heads of state address the opening sessions, which bring together
representatives of nearly 200 nations (for a list of member states see
Appendix C), many wearing national garb. Then the members get
down to the substantive work, which lasts until mid-December.

The UN Charter assigns the General Assembly responsibility for
considering any issue that relates to a UN body or agency. The assem-

bly commissions studies about international law, human rights, and all forms of international social, economic, cultural, and educational cooperation. It controls the purse strings, approves budgets, and decides how much each member state should contribute. It also elects the rotating members of the Security Council, as well as the members of the Economic and Social Council (ECOSOC) and the Trusteeship Council. In collaboration with the Security Council, it elects the judges of the International Court of Justice and appoints the Secretary General. Under some conditions the Security Council may ask the GA to meet in special session, and such sessions can also be requested by a majority of member states. Issues deemed more pressing may warrant an emergency special session of the assembly, convened on twenty-four hours' notice at the request of the Security Council or a majority of member states.

Despite these weighty responsibilities, the GA's resolutions have no legally binding force and derive their authority solely as acts of the world community.

Procedures

A two-tier system governs voting. Important matters like budgets and admission of new members require a two-thirds majority vote to pass, whereas others need only a simple majority. If, as often happens, the leadership can establish a consensus on a given matter, a formal vote may not even be needed.

General Assembly affairs are marked by a consuming passion for giving every member state some part of the action. There is a strong feeling that everyone should participate in as many decisions, committees, and issues as possible. The parliamentary and administrative structure of the assembly reflects and embodies this need.

At the beginning of each new General Assembly session, the members elect a president, twenty-one vice presidents (yes, twenty-one!), and the heads of the six Main Committees that run most of the assembly. Regional and national rivalries feed the politically charged voting for these positions. To keep peace among members, formal and

From the UN Charter

ARTICLE 11

1. The General Assembly may consider the general principles of co-operation in the maintenance of international peace and security, including the principles governing disarmament and the regulation of armaments, and may make recommendations with regard to such principles to the Members or to the Security Council or to both.

2. The General Assembly may discuss any questions relating to the maintenance of international peace and security brought before it by any Member of the United Nations, or by the Security Council, or by a state which is not a Member of the United Nations in accordance with Article 35, paragraph 2, and, except as provided in Article 12, may make recommendations with regard to any such questions to the state or states concerned or to the Security Council or to both. Any such question on which action is necessary shall be referred to the Security Council by the General Assembly either before or after discussion. . . .

informal mechanisms ensure that the prerogatives and rewards of office are spread around. The presidency, for example, is rotated annually according to geographical region. If an Eastern European member state has the presidency one year, it must go to another region the next year. Because no one can be president of the GA two years in succession, it is impossible to have continuity in the office. This produces a certain inefficiency that is tolerated because of a perceived greater good.

Main Committees

The speeches and debates of the full General Assembly often make good media events and excellent political theater, but they are not

ARTICLE 13

1. The General Assembly shall initiate studies and make recommendations for the purpose of:
   a. promoting international co-operation in the political field and encouraging the progressive development of international law and its codification;
   b. promoting international co-operation in the economic, social, cultural, educational, and health fields, and assisting in the realization of human rights and fundamental freedoms for all without distinction as to race, sex, language, or religion. . . .

ARTICLE 17

1. The General Assembly shall consider and approve the budget of the Organization.
2. The expenses of the Organization shall be borne by the Members as apportioned by the General Assembly.
3. The General Assembly shall consider and approve any financial and budgetary arrangements with specialized agencies referred to in Article 57 and shall examine the administrative budgets of such specialized agencies with a view to making recommendations to the agencies concerned.

necessarily effective means of examining issues in depth and arriving at solutions. For that, the GA relies heavily on a clutch of committees: a General Committee, a Credentials Committee, and six Main Committees. Committees are common in legislatures worldwide because they enable many issues to be carefully examined simultaneously. In the US Congress, committees consider legislation in the form of "bills," which become "laws" when passed by the full House and Senate and signed by the President. General Assembly committees call their bills "resolutions." Each committee deliberates during the assembly session, votes on issues by simple majority, and sends its

Symbolic Logic

"The General Assembly unfortunately has become a fairly useless body. At the symbolic level, it represents universality at the UN. All countries of the world virtually, even Switzerland now, are members of it. But the way it works has meant that it rarely takes meaningful decisions, and it takes so many un-meaningful decisions that it has been largely written off by the media. There's one significant function of the General Assembly. It serves as the umbrella for treaty negotiations on everything from the International Criminal Court to treaties on climate change, biodiversity, you name it. The treaties matter tremendously in the conduct of international relations."
—David Malone

draft resolutions to the full GA for a final vote. General Assembly resolutions, even when passed by vote, remain "resolutions" and, unlike laws, are not legally binding.

The General Committee consists of the GA president, the twenty-one vice presidents, and the heads of the other committees. The Credentials Committee is responsible for deciding who are the proper, accredited GA representatives of each member state. This is usually a pro forma matter except when a nation is divided by civil war and two delegations claim the same seat. Then this normally unobtrusive committee becomes the scene of intense politicking and high emotions. A recent example of a disputed delegation involved Afghanistan, where the sitting delegation was challenged by the Taliban regime when it seized power. The Credentials Committee listened to presentations by both sides and then "deferred consideration," effectively confirming the old delegation without explicitly rejecting the claim of the other one. Such sidestepping, or action through inaction, is a classic political ploy.

Each of the six Main Committees has both a number and a name, and either may be used to describe it, but insiders usually use only the number. First Committee (Disarmament and International Security)

considers resolutions about global security and weapons of mass destruction, as well as more conventional weapons. Second Committee
(Economic and Financial) is responsible for examining economic and
social development and international trade, including the reduction of
barriers that prevent developing nations from reaching their full export potential. Third Committee (Social, Humanitarian, and Cultural)
is concerned with a hodgepodge of issues ranging from disaster relief
to human rights. It also deals with international crime, including
drugs, human trafficking, and money-laundering, as well as government and business corruption. Fourth Committee (Special Political
and Decolonization), despite its name, no longer addresses decolonization because there are no more colonies. Instead, it has made peacekeeping its primary mission. The committee also has oversight of the
United Nations Relief and Works Agency for Palestine Refugees in
the Near East (UNRWA). Fifth Committee (Administrative and Budgetary) oversees the UN's fiscal affairs, and it drafts the resolutions for
the general budget that the GA votes on. Sixth Committee (Legal)
oversees important legal issues, such as human cloning, international
terrorism, and war crimes.

The World's Conference Host

The General Assembly also hosts conferences, many of which have
played a key role in guiding the work of the UN since its inception
(which occurred at a conference in San Francisco in 1945). Since
1994, the UN has held thirty-four conferences (as of May 2002)
around the world on a variety of issues. Recent high-profile meetings on development issues have put long-term, difficult problems
like poverty and environmental degradation at the top of the global
agenda. In an effort to make the meetings into global forums that will
shape the future of major issues, the UN has encouraged participation
of thousands of nongovernmental organizations (NGOs), experts, and
others not formally associated with the UN.

A landmark conference that is continuing to redefine the UN's
mission is the Millennium Summit in September 2000 and its

Annual Days and Weeks

The UN year is marked by nearly sixty days and weeks that call attention to important world issues and provide the occasion for educational and public events both inside and outside the United Nations.

21 February—International Mother Language Day
 8 March—United Nations Day for Women's Rights and International Peace
21 March—International Day for the Elimination of Racial Discrimination
21 March—Beginning Week of Solidarity with the Peoples Struggling Against Racism and Racial Discrimination
22 March—World Day for Water
23 March—World Meteorological Day
 7 April—World Health Day
23 April—World Book and Copyright Day
 3 May—World Press Freedom Day
15 May—International Day of Families
17 May—World Telecommunication Day
22 May—International Day for Biological Diversity
25 May—Beginning Week of Solidarity with the Peoples of Non-Self-Governing Territories
31 May—World No-Tobacco Day
 4 June—International Day of Innocent Children Victims of Aggression
 5 June—World Environment Day
17 June—World Day to Combat Desertification and Drought
20 June—World Refugee Day
23 June—United Nations Public Service Day
26 June—International Day Against Drug Abuse and Illicit Trafficking
26 June—International Day in Support of Victims of Torture
   July—International Day of Cooperatives (first Saturday of July)
11 July—World Population Day
 9 August—International Day of the World's Indigenous People
12 August—International Youth Day
23 August—International Day for the Remembrance of the Slave Trade and Its Abolition

8 September—International Literacy Day

16 September—International Day for the Preservation of the Ozone Layer

21 September—International Day of Peace

September—World Maritime Day (during last week of September)

1 October—International Day of Older Persons

4–10 October—World Space Week

5 October—World Teachers' Day

October—World Habitat Day (first Monday of October)

October—International Day for Natural Disaster Reduction (second Wednesday of October)

9 October—World Post Day

10 October—World Mental Health Day

16 October—World Food Day

17 October—International Day for the Eradication of Poverty

24 October—United Nations Day

24 October—World Development Information Day

24–30 October—Disarmament Week

6 November—International Day for Preventing the Exploitation of the Environment in War and Armed Conflict

16 November—International Day for Tolerance

20 November—Africa Industrialization Day

20 November—Universal Children's Day

21 November—World Television Day

25 November—International Day for the Elimination of Violence Against Women

29 November—International Day of Solidarity with the Palestinian People

1 December—World AIDS Day

2 December—International Day for the Abolition of Slavery

3 December—International Day of Disabled Persons

5 December—International Volunteer Day for Economic and Social Development

7 December—International Civil Aviation Day

10 December—Human Rights Day

18 December—International Migrants Day

World leaders attending the UN Millennium Summit held Sept. 6–8, 2000.
United Nations photo by Terry J. Deglau/Eastman Kodak.

accompanying Millennium Assembly (Sept. 12–Dec. 23, 2000). The
lofty Millennium Development Goals, which all member states have
agreed to meet by 2015, include:

Eradicate extreme poverty and hunger
Achieve universal primary education
Promote gender equality and empower women
Reduce child mortality
Improve maternal health
Combat HIV/AIDS, malaria, and other diseases
Ensure environmental sustainability
Develop a global partnership for development

Millennium Assembly delegates also took a special look at the problems in Africa, particularly the HIV/AIDS crisis.

Although the Millennium Summit was a landmark event for the
UN, it has attracted less press attention than the so-called Monterey
Conference held in March 2002. Monterey's official name, the Inter-
national Conference on Financing for Development, holds a clue to

The General Assembly Hall, September 1990. UN photo 176114 by John Isaac.

the meeting's high public visibility, because it addressed fundamental issues of globalization that raise strong emotions among governments, the business community, and NGOs concerned about perceived inequities in the internationalized economy of the past decade. Some 50 government heads joined business leaders, agency directors, and representatives of civil society to examine ways of achieving a new global approach to financing development. A series of roundtables enabled more than 800 members of various stakeholder constituencies to express their views while heads of government and of key organizations like the World Bank and the World Trade Organization listened. It was quite a show.

Some Criticism

The assembly's culture favors moving through consensus, which takes time when nearly 200 delegates are involved. Nancy Soderberg and other insiders accustomed to the relative speed and decisiveness of the Security Council chafe at the inefficient and polarized approach in the GA: "It's very difficult to be in the General Assembly because everything is done by consensus so it's the lowest common denominator of 191 different countries, which is a pretty low standard." This means that the assembly effectively cedes decisive action to the Security Council. As Soderberg says: "Everyone pretends that they don't want to be run by the Security Council, but the key agenda is run by the council. The assembly can put out resolutions on laudatory, amorphous goals, but if you're really going to have an impact and do things, do it through the Security Council."

Critics also complain about the GA's tendency to form cliques and blocs and stay with them even after they have outlived their purposes. Soderberg accuses the blocs of being out of step with current realities. "Look at the Nonaligned Movement," she says, referring to a coalition established during the cold war. "What are they nonaligned against now? There is no alignment, which means that they are really trying to oppose the US more often than not, which makes no sense." Richard Holbrooke shares her exasperation. The Nonaligned Movement and the G-77 (a group of third-world nations) do tremendous damage because they "just don't serve the interests of most of their members. They are two groups which are pulled by old-school politics." Compounding the problem is the passion for making speeches. Holbrooke describes the GA as "a forum for people to make speeches. It started off as a wonderful dream for people to exchange ideas. There is nothing that the GA does that is important," he claims, except for some of the speeches in the annual fall session.

CHAPTER 8

Coordinating to Fight International Terrorism

The spread of terrorism is a threat to the very foundations of the United Nations, and to the spirit of its Charter. Over the years, the organization has played an important role in establishing a legal framework for the eradication of terrorism through one of its basic roles: the codification of international law—more specifically through twelve United Nations antiterrorist conventions and protocols. These conventions must be strictly observed and effectively implemented if terrorism is to be defeated.

—Kofi Annan, Secretary General of the United Nations

After the September 11 attacks in the US, the General Assembly held a five-day debate on what to do about international terrorism. Not that this was a new issue for the delegates. Dealing with international terrorism has been on the UN's agenda for many years, but it did not claim major attention until the 1990s. Terrorist attacks have long been a part of life for the citizens in some nations, notably the Israelis, Spanish (Basques), British (Northern Ireland), Filipinos (Muslim separatists), and others. The attacks became more frequent and bloody during the 1990s, after the end of the cold war saw the outbreak of conflicts—in Chechnya, for example—that fanned hatreds. Meanwhile, the intensification of economic globalization made national borders more porous

Secretary General Kofi Annan speaks at the UN Peace Bell Ceremony, which was postponed for three days out of respect for the victims of the September 11 terrorist attacks against the United States. UN/DPI photo by Eskinder Debebe.

while hugely increasing people's mobility, so that it was easier for terrorists to move both money and weapons. The attacks of September 11 placed the United States at the head of terror-afflicted nations and helped raise international awareness about the urgency of the threat.

An Emerging Consensus

A striking aspect of recent anti-terrorist deliberations is that the major powers all seem to be generally on the same page. The Security Council's P5 publicly and officially agree that only through joint efforts can they hope to stop or reduce terrorism. The US anti-terrorist position became especially visible several years ago, once Osama bin Laden emerged as leader of his Al Qaeda network and began targeting American government and military facilities. Late in 1999, at US urging, the Security Council passed a resolution requiring the Taliban government in Afghanistan to give up bin Laden. It also imposed limited sanctions as a goad to the Taliban, but to no avail. Soon after, the council passed Resolution 1269, which pledged a "common fight against terrorists everywhere" and specified that member states should share information and refuse to provide a safe haven to terrorists. Since then the pace has quickened. At the end of 1999, the General Assembly voted to adopt the International Convention for the Suppression of the Financing of Terrorism. This convention makes it a crime to participate in raising funds for terrorist activity, even if no terrorist act ensues. One day after 9/11, the Security Council officially decreed, for the first time, that acts of international terrorism are threats to international peace and security.

The events of September 11 pushed the council to act quickly in creating a broad resolution aimed at cutting off all support to international terrorists. Resolution 1373, approved on September 28, 2001, requires that all member states prevent their citizens and banking institutions from providing money to terrorists or give terrorists safe haven, and it requires each member state to report steps it has taken to the Security Council's new Counterterrorism Committee. The US has submitted a detailed report, which it hopes will become a blueprint for other nations in fighting terrorism.

Meanwhile, the General Assembly has been deliberating on its own anti-terrorism measure, a comprehensive resolution designed to augment the dozen international anti-terrorism conventions now on the books. As you might expect, the assembly's diverse membership has struggled to find consensus. One area of dispute is how to define terrorism. Delegates from some Middle Eastern and Asian states argue the need to distinguish between terrorism, which they agreed is an evil, and acts done in the name of ethnic or national self-determination, which they view as legitimate. The US and its friends, however, have branded such distinctions as unacceptable.

Security Council Resolution 1373 (2001)

Adopted by the Security Council at its 4385th meeting, on 28 September 2001

The Security Council,

Reaffirming its resolutions 1269 (1999) of 19 October 1999 and 1368 (2001) of 12 September 2001,

Reaffirming also its unequivocal condemnation of the terrorist attacks which took place in New York, Washington, D.C. and Pennsylvania on 11 September 2001, and expressing its determination to prevent all such acts,

Reaffirming further that such acts, like any act of international terrorism, constitute a threat to international peace and security,

Reaffirming the inherent right of individual or collective self-defence as recognized by the Charter of the United Nations as reiterated in resolution 1368 (2001),

Reaffirming the need to combat by all means, in accordance with the Charter of the United Nations, threats to international peace and security caused by terrorist acts,

Deeply concerned by the increase, in various regions of the world, of acts of terrorism motivated by intolerance or extremism,

Calling on States to work together urgently to prevent and suppress terrorist acts, including through increased cooperation and full implementation of the relevant international conventions relating to terrorism,

Recognizing the need for States to complement international cooperation by taking additional measures to prevent and suppress, in their territories through all lawful means, the financing and preparation of any acts of terrorism,

Reaffirming the principle established by the General Assembly in its declaration of October 1970 (resolution 2625 (XXV)) and reiterated by the Security Council in its resolution 1189 (1998) of 13 August 1998, namely that every State has the duty to refrain from organizing, instigating, assisting or participating in terrorist acts in another State or acquiescing in organized activities within its territory directed towards the commission of such acts,

Acting under Chapter VII of the Charter of the United Nations,

1. Decides that all States shall:

(a) Prevent and suppress the financing of terrorist acts;

(b) Criminalize the wilful provision or collection, by any means, directly or indirectly, of funds by their nationals or in their territories with the intention that the funds should be used, or in the knowledge that they are to be used, in order to carry out terrorist acts;

(c) Freeze without delay funds and other financial assets or economic resources of persons who commit, or attempt to commit, terrorist acts or participate in or facilitate the commission of terrorist acts; of entities owned or controlled directly or indirectly by such persons; and of persons and entities acting on behalf of, or at the direction of such persons and entities, including funds derived or generated from property owned or controlled directly or indirectly by such persons and associated persons and entities;

(d) Prohibit their nationals or any persons and entities within their territories from making any funds, financial assets or economic resources or financial or other related services available, directly or indirectly, for the benefit of persons who commit or attempt to commit or facilitate or participate in the commission of terrorist acts, of entities owned or controlled, directly or indirectly, by such persons and of persons and entities acting on behalf of or at the direction of such persons;

2. Decides also that all States shall:

(a) Refrain from providing any form of support, active or passive, to entities or persons involved in terrorist acts, including by suppressing recruitment of members of terrorist groups and eliminating the supply of weapons to terrorists;

(b) Take the necessary steps to prevent the commission of terrorist acts, including by provision of early warning to other States by exchange of information;

(c) Deny safe haven to those who finance, plan, support, or commit terrorist acts, or provide safe havens;

(d) Prevent those who finance, plan, facilitate or commit terrorist acts from using their respective territories for those purposes against other States or their citizens;

(e) Ensure that any person who participates in the financing, planning, preparation or perpetration of terrorist acts or in supporting terrorist acts is brought to justice and ensure that, in addition to any other measures against them, such terrorist acts are established as serious criminal offences in domestic laws and regulations and that the punishment duly reflects the seriousness of such terrorist acts;

(f) Afford one another the greatest measure of assistance in connection with criminal investigations or criminal proceedings relating to the financing or support of terrorist acts, including assistance in obtaining evidence in their possession necessary for the proceedings;

(g) Prevent the movement of terrorists or terrorist groups by effective border controls and controls on issuance of identity papers and travel documents, and through measures for preventing counterfeiting, forgery or fraudulent use of identity papers and travel documents;

3. Calls upon all States to:

(a) Find ways of intensifying and accelerating the exchange of operational information, especially regarding actions or movements of terrorist persons or networks; forged or falsified travel documents; traffic in arms, explosives or sensitive materials; use of communications technologies by terrorist groups; and the threat posed by the possession of weapons of mass destruction by terrorist groups;

(b) Exchange information in accordance with international and domestic law and cooperate on administrative and judicial matters to prevent the commission of terrorist acts;

(c) Cooperate, particularly through bilateral and multilateral arrangements and agreements, to prevent and suppress terrorist attacks and take action against perpetrators of such acts;

(d) Become parties as soon as possible to the relevant international conventions and protocols relating to terrorism, including the International Convention for the Suppression of the Financing of Terrorism of 9 December 1999;

(e) Increase cooperation and fully implement the relevant international conventions and protocols relating to terrorism and Security Council resolutions 1269 (1999) and 1368 (2001);

(f) Take appropriate measures in conformity with the relevant provisions of national and international law, including international standards of human rights, before granting refugee status, for the purpose of ensuring that the asylum-seeker has not planned, facilitated or participated in the commission of terrorist acts;

(g) Ensure, in conformity with international law, that refugee status is not abused by the perpetrators, organizers or facilitators of terrorist acts, and that claims of political motivation are not recognized as grounds for refusing requests for the extradition of alleged terrorists;

4. Notes with concern the close connection between international terrorism and transnational organized crime, illicit drugs, money-laundering, illegal arms-trafficking, and illegal movement of nuclear, chemical, biological and other potentially deadly materials, and in this regard emphasizes the need to enhance coordination of efforts on national, subregional, regional and international levels in order to strengthen a global response to this serious challenge and threat to international security;

5. Declares that acts, methods, and practices of terrorism are contrary to the purposes and principles of the United Nations and that knowingly financing, planning and inciting terrorist acts are also contrary to the purposes and principles of the United Nations;

6. Decides to establish, in accordance with rule 28 of its provisional rules of procedure, a Committee of the Security Council, consisting of all the members of the Council, to monitor implementation of this resolution, with the assistance of appropriate expertise, and calls upon all States to report to the Committee, no later than 90 days from the date of adoption of this resolution and thereafter according to a timetable to be proposed by the Committee, on the steps they have taken to implement this resolution;

7. Directs the Committee to delineate its tasks, submit a work programme within 30 days of the adoption of this resolution, and to consider the support it requires, in consultation with the Secretary-General;

8. Expresses its determination to take all necessary steps in order to ensure the full implementation of this resolution, in accordance with its responsibilities under the Charter;

9. Decides to remain seized of this matter.

The UN System at Work

Although the Security Council and the General Assembly lead in defining and addressing the threat of international terrorism through debates and resolutions, they receive assistance from a variety of UN bodies. One of them is the UN Office on Drugs and Crime (UNODC), an umbrella office for programs and entities directed at all aspects of international criminal activity, including terrorism.

The Vienna-based UNODC has two broad program centers—the Drug Program and the Crime Program. (The Drug Program is discussed in Chapter 26.) The Crime Program directs the Global Program Against Terrorism, established in 2002, which works closely with the Security Council's Counter-Terrorism Committee, to encourage international cooperation against terrorism. The Crime Program also helps member states ratify and implement UN conventions relating to crimes, narcotics, and terrorism, such as the Convention against Transnational Crime. Adopted by the General Assembly at the Millennium Summit in November 2000, the convention went into force in September 2003.

In the aftermath of September 11, the International Atomic Energy Agency (IAEA) has led the conversation about preventing terrorists from using nuclear weapons. It is the world's forum for discussing, debating, and regulating the peaceful, and sometimes not so peaceful, use of atomic energy. The IAEA's director, Mohamed El Baradei, noted in a recent press account that because terrorists were willing to take their own lives when committing their violence, the nuclear threat was very serious. Since 1993, the IAEA has identified 175 cases of trafficking in nuclear material, but only a handful have involved weapons-grade uranium or plutonium. The IAEA operates the Emergency Response Center, the world's only international response system capable of reacting quickly to the effects of a nuclear terrorist attack.

Terrorists have other weapons available should they lack enriched uranium or plutonium. In 1995, for example, members of a Japanese

As of December 2001, the US had signed and enacted legislation to implement 10 of the 12 UN anti-terrorism conventions and protocols:

1. Convention on Offenses and Certain Other Acts Committed On Board Aircraft, 1963 (Tokyo Convention)
2. Convention for the Suppression of the Unlawful Seizure of Aircraft, 1970 (Hague Convention)
3. Convention for the Suppression of Unlawful Acts Against the Safety of Civil Aviation, 1971 (Montreal Convention)
4. Convention on the Prevention and Punishment of Crimes Against Internationally Protected Persons, 1973
5. International Convention Against the Taking of Hostages, 1979 (Hostages Convention)
6. Convention on the Physical Protection of Nuclear Material, 1980
7. Protocol for the Suppression of Unlawful Acts of Violence at Airports Serving International Civil Aviation, 1988, supplementary to the Convention for the Suppression of Unlawful Acts Against the Safety of Civil Aviation
8. Convention for the Suppression of Unlawful Acts Against the Safety of Maritime Navigation, 1988
9. Protocol for the Suppression of Unlawful Acts Against the Safety of Fixed Platforms Located on the Continental Shelf, 1988
10. Convention on the Marking of Plastic Explosives for the Purpose of Detection, 1991

The government hoped soon to ratify the International Convention for the Suppression of Terrorist Bombings and the International Convention for the Suppression of the Financing of Terrorism. (*Source:* US Department of State, *US Report to the UN Counterterrorism Committee,* 2001, 14–15.)

cult killed a dozen people by releasing the deadly nerve gas Sarin in the Tokyo subway. Information about chemical weapons—like nerve gases—and countermeasures is available from the Organization for the Prohibition of Chemical Weapons (OPCW). Established to implement the Chemical Weapons Convention, which entered into force in 1997, the OPCW tracks the international movement of materials that can be used to make these weapons. The convention prohibits states from using chemical weapons and makes it a crime for citizens to do anything that violates the convention.

It is illegal to use a biological agent like anthrax in war, according to the 1972 Convention on the Prohibition of the Development, Production, and Stockpiling of Bacteriological (Biological) and Toxin Weapons and on Their Destruction. But all nations have not yet signed the convention, which in any case does not include enforcement mechanisms. This is an area of great concern to UN officials. Meanwhile, the World Health Organization (WHO), a UN specialized agency, can provide information about the identification and treatment of most biologically induced illnesses.

For many years, terrorists have used commercial airliners as targets for destruction or as pawns in blackmail efforts. The International Civil Aviation Organization (ICAO) is the world's leader in setting policies to prevent such attacks. Created in 1944, the ICAO does this as part of its general mandate to develop international standards for aviation safety and efficiency. An ICAO ministerial conference in 2002 that looked at the effectiveness of anti-terrorism airline regulations drew representatives from 154 governments and approved a new security plan that includes regular audits of airport security.

Protection of people and goods at sea is the concern of the International Maritime Organization (IMO), created in 1958 to help governments more safely and effectively control ships engaged in international trade. Most UN members have ratified the United Nations Convention for the Suppression of Unlawful Acts Against the Safety of Maritime Navigation and its Protocol for the Suppression of Unlawful Acts Against the Safety of Fixed Platforms Located on the Continental Shelf.

The vulnerability of the mails to terrorism was demonstrated vividly in fall 2001, when members of Congress and others received letters purposely contaminated with anthrax spores. As long ago as 1989, a UN specialized agency, the Universal Postal Union (UPU), created a Postal Security Action Group to examine and publicize mail-related security issues. The UPU helps national postal systems collaborate with one another to ensure that mail travels efficiently and reliably across the globe. Out of sight and mind of most of us, it sets the rules that govern what kind of mail we can send abroad and how the letters and packages will be handled. Its world postal security network offers postal authorities advice and training about preventing dangerous materials from being sent through the mails. And, although the network was originally aimed at drug-trafficking, money-laundering, fraud, and child pornography, it has obvious relevance to acts of terrorism.

Terrorism and Failed States

"An area where we do spend a lot of our time is the issue of failed states. The breeding ground for terrorism or proliferation or any other manner of ills of this world, whether it's narcotics trafficking or other forms of antisocial behavior, is more likely to develop in a country whose institutions have broken down. My speechwriter, Bob Earle, invented a wonderful phrase when we first spoke of Afghanistan. He said Afghanistan wasn't promoting state-sponsored terrorism; rather, Afghanistan was a terrorist-sponsored state. You break down law and order, you destroy the economic system and existing institutions, and then a criminal enterprise moves in and takes the place over and uses the country for its own purposes. That's what Osama bin Laden did when he moved in on the Taliban and used Afghanistan for his own purposes. We at the UN have an interest in states not failing and we spend a lot of time dealing with states that are threatened in that way."
—John Negroponte, US Ambassador to the UN

CHAPTER 9

The UN Village

The amount of psychology in diplomacy is remarkable. States behave very much as human beings. It is very ego driven, I would say. We want to be there, we want to be where decisions are taken.
—Danilo Türk, Former Slovenian Ambassador to the UN and
Assistant Secretary General for Political Affairs

The United Nations is known for operating in ways that often seem complicated and convoluted. The Secretariat's administrators have their intricate procedures and protocols and their proper, not always straight and narrow, channels. The same is true in the General Assembly, where red tape decorates resolutions, studies, reports, and memoranda. In the many related bodies like the World Bank or agencies like UNESCO, a passion for creating and filing paper does occasionally obscure the central point of the organization.

But just as often the UN is as simple and straightforward a place as can be imagined, because, as David Malone notes, "people really matter at the UN." Many experts who look at the UN's structure, procedures, and resolutions don't realize that "anything that happens at the UN happens because of certain individuals."

Malone calculates that "at any given time, out of a hundred and ninety ambassadors, about thirty-five control the game. Within the Security Council four or five ambassadors at any given time are dominant, perhaps a few more counting the nonpermanent ones. This is also true in each of the General Assembly committees. In the Secretariat it's true." So, if you know those thirty-five key people, you can do anything. And if you don't, forget it.

When trying to understand the UN, it's also important not to confuse administrative problems with issues of governance and decision-making. When talk turns into decision and action, the procedures can be very different from what bureaucrats are accustomed to, and often that difference is the reason things get done. Governance and decision-making often involve levels of persuasion, guile, and gall that one would find in a novel or movie about Wall Street.

The Village

Think of a small town, where decisions are made by groups of key people who know one another and often socialize while standing at street corners or sipping coffee at a café. In fact, this is exactly how Richard Holbrooke describes his experience as US Permanent Rep under President Clinton. Looking back on those sixteen months in New York City, he remembers a place that he calls the UN Village, located on the Upper East Side, "with its own language and time zone, where 'demand' means 'ask,' 'strong' means 'not so strong' and 'severe' means 'not so severe' and 'urges' means 'begs.' All a different lingo. Thousands of people live here who have very little interaction with the rest of the city." The village works through small groups, formal or informal, endless meetings, caucuses, speeches, and meals. "Food is probably the thing that holds the UN together," notes Holbrooke. "Boy, do those guys like to eat!"

The current US Permanent Rep, John Negroponte, also operates in the UN Village. "I've called on a hundred and fourteen delegates," he remarked recently when asked about his first few months at the UN. "I'm going to call on everyone that I'm allowed to call on. The diplo-

matic practice is that if you arrived after another delegate, then you go
and call on them. If they've arrived after you have, then they go and see
you. The new kid on the block comes around to see you."

Negroponte tries even harder to meet with regional groups "because the regional groups are where a lot of the business of the UN is
done." He visits with the European Union "once every six or eight
weeks" and with the South African Development Group, the Economic Council of West African States (ECOWAS), and others. "Meeting with" can often mean drinks or dinner, sometimes at the Waldorf
Astoria.

As a suave and skilled professional diplomat, Negroponte tries to
avoid ruffling feathers. "We're diplomats, so whatever feelings people
may have they're going to be muted, guarded, and careful," he says. "I
think most diplomats feel that you can disagree without being dis-
agreeable. I think that's part of our work ethic, because otherwise you
could live in quite unbearable circumstances." Even when one must
take an unpopular position, he argues, one can try to do it respectfully
and courteously, and that's appreciated by the others.

Within the UN Village are "neighborhoods," some of them pretty
exclusive. Negroponte lives in one of the toniest, the Security Council.
"Most of my dealings are in the Security Council, which is a fairly
small and tight-knit group and we meet each other one way or another
every day. We get to know each other pretty well. And so there is a
certain camaraderie in the Security Council." He also has to spend
some time in that other part of town, the General Assembly, where
crowds of ordinary nations mill about, shouting and waving their
hands. "I think where the nerves sometimes get a little frayed around
the edges is in some of these big General Assembly special sessions,
particularly when you have to reach consensus on a document. Nerves
can get frayed and you have these marathon meetings that go on until
eight in the morning, and you have NGOs in the bleachers which are
pushing single-minded positions. But even there, particularly if you
can succeed in achieving consensus, if you can reach consensus on a
document, I think there's always a huge sense of relief even amongst

Nancy E. Soderberg was alternate US representative to the UN, with the rank of Ambassador, from 1997–2000. Previously she was deputy assistant to President Clinton for national security affairs. She is currently Vice President of the International Crisis Group.

those who were opposed to positions we had. They can say to themselves, at least we produced something at the end of this."

Like all villages, this one has its cliques and factions. For one thing, the population is very male, a sort of diplomatic stag party of political incorrectness. (By contrast, women do very well in many other parts of the UN: in 2000, American women represented over 53 percent of all Americans in professional and senior positions in the UN Secretariat and 44 percent of Americans in all UN agencies.)

The few women who crash the party have described the experience in various ways. Madeleine Albright, who was US Permanent Representative, remembers the thrill of being not just a woman in that environment but "the woman who represents the United States," the dominant power.

Other women representatives may not feel the power rush yet recall the special quality of life at a men's club. Nancy Soderberg remembers old-fashioned gallantry. "Being a woman there is interesting, particularly if you are on the Security Council, because there are no women on the Security Council." She enjoyed the men's attention. "One of the things that I just loved, being a young woman on the council, is that chivalry really does live there. They are so gentlemanly and just wonderful. At times they come up and kiss your hand and everyone stands up for you." Try that in the US Senate!

Security Council Politics

The UN Village is especially visible on the Security Council, which is a small body that constitutes an elite club within the UN system. Most member states regard participation on the council as an honor, but not everyone sees it that way.

John Negroponte recalls that it took a while for Mexico to make up its mind about seeking a council seat because of concerns among many Mexicans about a no-win situation: "If we agree with the US, then that will be taken for granted, and if we disagree with the US, that will hurt us in our bilateral relationship with the US." Newly elected president Vicente Fox and others took the opposite tack, maintaining that Mexico needed to be more visible on the world stage and not worry about how the audience would react. Mexicans at the UN constantly asked Negroponte, "Will you hold it against Mexico if we take positions against the US or at odds with the US?" Negroponte replied with diplomatic aplomb, "Everything we do is going to be in the context of an excellent bilateral relationship . . . we may have our differences, but it's a crucial relationship to us and it's going to remain that and we're going to deal with Mexico accordingly."

Mexico has by no means been the only nation to hesitate before deciding whether to run for election to the Security Council. When the newly minted nation of Slovenia, once part of Yugoslavia, took stock of its diplomatic situation, one of the first matters considered was possible candidacy for the Security Council. Danilo Türk was Slovenia's Ambassador to the UN during the 1990s (and Security Council President in August 1998). "I thought Slovenia would make a good show in the Security Council," he says, but that was not the universal opinion either in the UN or in Slovenia itself. "There was a debate whether or not we need that. Membership in the Security Council brings exposure to have to deal with issues which are very politically contested. It was not an easy decision, and I presented pluses and minuses." One of the pluses was that membership would strengthen the new nation's profile in the world community.

Finally Slovenia decided to throw its hat in the ring for the elections scheduled in 1997. But first the government had to decide which voting bloc it should run in. As always in the UN, a quota system ensures that each world region will have representation. In any given year, a certain number of places will open up for the "Western Europe

Danilo Türk is UN Assistant Secretary General for Political Affairs and was Slovenia's first Ambassador to the UN (1992–2000). In addition he served on the Security Council from 1998 to 1999. He is a lawyer and a former academic.

and Others" bloc (WEOG) or for the "Latin American" bloc, for example, and countries in those regions will compete with one another for a seat. Sometimes the countries of a region will agree who should be elected to the open slots. Other times the countries will engage in a genuine political campaign involving arm-twisting, alliances, and occasional back-stabbing.

The politics can get especially nasty if one nation finds the candidacy of another obnoxious. For example, in fall 2000, three Western European countries were fighting for two slots. According to news reports, Norway and Italy were "wining and dining decision-makers in New York and elsewhere," while the third candidate, Ireland, was appealing to developing countries in the General Assembly, "stressing its poor, former-colonial roots as proof that it understands their needs." The United States was not taking sides but was concentrating instead on backing an African nation, Mauritius, in order to prevent Sudan, which was under Security Council sanctions, from becoming a Security Council member. The US accused Sudan of massive human rights abuses and of having links with terrorists. African diplomats, however, were said to resent US strong-arm tactics, while European diplomats were claiming that the US could have persuaded Sudan to withdraw its candidacy by offering to lift its own sanctions against Sudan. But the US persisted and was rewarded when the General Assembly elected Mauritius, in the fourth round of voting, as one of five new Security Council members to serve in 2001 and 2002.

Danilo Türk did not face quite such high-powered politics when he guided Slovenia through its Security Council candidacy, but he did have to decide whether to campaign for the slot of "Western Europe and Others" or "Eastern Europe." "Initially we didn't want to be a

member of the eastern European group. We said we are geographi-
cally west of Vienna, we didn't think automatically that there should
be any linkage between the former Yugoslavia membership in the east
European group and Slovenian membership in the same group."
Later the Slovenians changed their minds, "because we thought, it is
important to get elected." They decided in 1996 to join the Eastern
European group, "where it is easier to get elected than the western
because the competition is not as tough." Valuable time had passed,
however, and there were two other candidates for the seat, Belarus and
Macedonia. "Usually member states announce their candidature five
years in advance, in some cases, ten or fifteen years in advance, and
they campaign gradually. The last two years they campaign very in-
tensely. Of course if the seat is not contested, there is no campaign but
even then they have to talk to other members because they have to get
two-thirds of the entire membership. We came very late and there
were two other candidates, but I had to do it. Because if I didn't, I
would be asked, Where were you, what were you doing? Belarus withdrew at last minute, a couple of days before elections because they had
no chance. We defeated the remaining candidate. So that's how Slovenia became a member of the Security Council."

And it was worth it, says Türk, if only for all the international
publicity. "We discovered that half of what was important internationally about Slovenia related to the Security Council in those two years
[1998–99]. For a small country, this is an incredible exposure."

Türk makes a bigger, more interesting argument when he observes
that smaller nations may not be as bound by rigid policies and positions as larger ones, giving them the opportunity to orchestrate some
creative diplomacy where otherwise there might be conflict or confrontation. "If a country like Slovenia fails, it is no problem, but if a big
country fails with a proposal, that usually has political repercussions.
So small countries, nonpermanent members, can be constructive and
genuinely helpful members of the Security Council. They can afford
some imagination and experimentation. I always believed that. I never
thought that only permanent members count." David Malone largely
agrees. Although nonpermanent members vary enormously in qual-

A Diplomat Rates the Media

"The professionalism among the reporters at the UN is one of my big discoveries at the Security Council. They knew the background, knew what to quote, and they also knew how to formulate an opinion. It was always very clear what is quotation, what is opinion, so I could rely on the reports from the local press. Sometimes things got tricky, on Iraq, on Kosovo. We had questions: What do you mean? Did you say that? And sometimes the one who comes to you with an accusation or interpretation can be trumped by the original report. So I took the reports from the newspaper or the press agency and said, 'Look that is what was reported, that is absolutely correct. It is your understanding or your explanation which creates a problem.' My respect for reporters grew exponentially as a result of such experiences. People who work here are very knowledgeable and are good reporters, so it's something that has to be respected."   —Danilo Türk

ity, "at any given time you have a number of high-quality delegations or ambassadors" who may function at a high level on the council.

Formally Informal or Informally Formal?

Once a member state becomes a player in a clique or faction, it needs to know the rules and procedures. One of the basic principles is that the most important business is done ostensibly in the open but actually in private. There's a reason why so many decisions, not just at the UN but in organizations all over the world, are made by a few people in a back room. Chances are that if the terms of the agreement were discussed in public, with all the constraints of touchy issues, no one would agree to anything significant. So a common arrangement at the UN is to begin a debate or discussion in a large public setting, like the Security Council chamber, and then, as the individual points become defined, break up into smaller, less public groups. Finally, a few

Between Acts

"You see another side of these guys when you get them out of the formal setting. Wang is very interesting. He's very quiet, but if you get him alone, he's very curious and down to earth and more open than other Chinese reps I've seen. You can actually have an argument with him about Tibet."   —Nancy Soderberg

people sitting at a table resolve the most contentious points, with no media presence and sometimes not even anyone taking notes.

In the Security Council, the opening discussions are referred to as the formals, and the subsequent less public ones as the informals. Nancy Soderberg came to regard the formal meetings as "just a staged show, there is just nothing that happens in them." Rather, the serious negotiations happen at the informals, "because you can't negotiate in a formal setting, you can't talk to people." Occasionally the formal setting is good for sending signals to another member, but nothing happens there. "For the most part, you go in, there's a briefing that nobody pays attention to, and everyone reads prepared statements and nothing happens."

Sometimes, though, even the informals are too formal for serious talk. "The informals are not so informal," says Soderberg. "It still is pretty formal because you have a chair who does everyone in order. It's really hard to have negotiations when you have to wait your turn." The actual decision may already have been made anyway. But where? "In the back room," says Soderberg.

Quids for Quos

There are few secrets in the UN Village. Everyone knows everyone else—not just their strengths and weaknesses but their quirks too, and their sensitive places where you don't touch unless you're prepared for a strong reaction. Surprises are still possible, though, especially when one member state, or group of states, steps across one of the invisible annoyance lines that surround every member like the isobars on a weather map.

China, for example, is known to be very ticklish on the question of Taiwan. But some Central American countries have long championed membership for Taiwan in the UN. Every year they introduce a resolution in the General Assembly to admit Taiwan, and every year it is defeated. "But it never fails to irritate the hell out of China," remarks David Malone. A few years ago, when Guatemala was ending its civil war and needed a UN peacekeeping operation, the Chinese vetoed it, "as a signal to Guatemala that they simply wouldn't stand for Guatemala continuing to participate in this effort to legitimize Taiwan at the UN." So the Guatemalans met privately with the Chinese, "negotiated a reformulation of the Guatemala position on Taiwan that satisfied the Chinese, and the Chinese veto was lifted about ten days later."

Malone recalls another awkward Taiwan moment that occurred when the UN was engaged in a "preventive" deployment in Macedonia. "After a change of government in Macedonia, this was in 1998, a new government cozied up to Taiwan and was alleged to have accepted significant financial aid from Taiwan. When the mandate renewal of the UN preventive deployment came up, China vetoed it. It was denounced by other members of the Security Council for doing so, but naturally the Macedonian government should have known this would be the outcome of its cozying up to Taiwan."

CHAPTER 10

Rights versus Sovereignty: The US and the International Criminal Court

Bush administration officials said today that the new International Criminal Court should expect no cooperation from the United States, and that its prosecutors would not be given any information from the United States to help them bring cases against any individuals.
— *New York Times*, May 7, 2002, report by Neil A. Lewis

To what degree can and should the UN infringe on national sovereignty in the pursuit of justice against those who grossly violate human rights? In Chapter 3 we saw Kofi Annan's strong endorsement of the claims of rights over sovereignty. Now we turn to another round in the debate, the establishment of the International Criminal Court (ICC), a permanent tribunal for trying cases involving military or government personnel accused of committing genocide, war crimes, and other crimes against humanity.

The UN is associated with two international courts that are easily conflated by the casual observer but in reality are so different that they seem to be operating in different worlds. The International Court of Justice, also known as the World Court, is one of the Six Principal Organs of the UN. It hears only those cases involving states, not individuals. It also gives advisory opinions on legal questions at the request of international organizations. Its fifteen judges, serving nine-year terms, are elected through a complicated procedure by the Security Council and the General Assembly. No two judges may be nationals of the same state. The World Court is a fixture of the UN system and hardly controversial.

The other court, the ICC, is not formally part of the UN (although it expresses values embedded in the UN Charter). This court has become very controversial, at least in the United States, where one Congressman actually introduced a bill that, if made into law, could have American troops invading Holland, our longtime partner in the North Atlantic Treaty Organization (NATO) and the seat of the court. The ICC is solely a criminal tribunal. Its prosecutors and eighteen judges are not part of the UN and are accountable only to the countries that ratify the Rome Statute (1998), which established the court. The contentious point is that the court has the authority to bring individuals to trial without needing permission from any individual or government.

The Need to End Impunity

The ICC is designed to end impunity, which means the ability to act illegally without worrying about being caught and prosecuted. This is a major concern because enforcement has not kept pace with the rapid growth of international human rights law during the past fifty years. Too many atrocities go unpunished.

The UN sees the ICC as a way of addressing a problem that, in a sense, the UN helped create through its decades of assisting in the writing and codification of international rights law. The Charter enjoins the UN to systematize international law as part of its goal of encouraging global peace, justice, and stability. Through conventions, treaties, and other documents, the UN has helped create a framework for civilized behavior in all aspects of life, including war and unrest. The International Law Commission is the body that does the actual drafting of text for international conventions.

Unfortunately, in recent decades a new wave of war crimes has appeared, as soldiers increasingly find themselves engaged in civil wars and other forms of internal conflict involving guerrillas, paramilitary groups, or civilians. An especially vicious situation appears when one ethnic group fights against another, and personal and group prejudices and hatreds take over. Genocide can result when the restraints of military training and moral limitations are forgotten. Until recently there were no international courts for trying persons accused of committing atrocities, except for special tribunals such as the one at Nuremberg after World War II. Most perpetrators of atrocities have been able to act with impunity, as long as they remain in power or can find exile or asylum in a friendly country.

During the past half century, however, world opinion has turned sharply against ignoring or protecting persons accused of atrocities. A good example is Chile's former strongman, General Augusto Pinochet, who negotiated an end to his rule with safeguards that enabled him to live in Chile with little fear of prosecution for complicity in committing state human rights crimes while he held power. But when he left the country for medical attention several years ago, he was arrested and brought to Spain, where he narrowly escaped a trial in a Spanish court for crimes against humanity. If there had existed a single, international body with acknowledged jurisdiction to try cases involving human rights abuses, it is possible Pinochet would have actually been brought to justice.

The ICC remedies this deficiency. If the country where the atrocity occurred cannot or will not conduct its own investigation and trial, as was the case with Chile's refusal to try Pinochet, the court can step in. The existence of the ICC means that the Security Council will no longer be the sole world body authorized to establish human rights tribunals. The council created the first such tribunal in 1993 to deal with massacres in the former Yugoslavia. Staffed by 1,200 employees and operating out of The Hague, it has taken into custody and is trying publicly indicted war criminals, including former Yugoslav president Slobodan Milosevic. In 1994 the Security Council established a tribunal to examine the genocide in Rwanda; it has a staff of approximately 900 and is based in Kigali, Rwanda. The two tribunals share a chief prosecutor, Carla del Ponte of Switzerland. In 2000, a special court was set up in Sierra Leone to try those accused of committing atrocities against civilians and attacking UN forces disarming and demobilizing the combatants after a civil war.

The US applauded the formation of the UN tribunals and has been their most generous donor. In 2000, for example, its assessed and voluntary contributions amounted to about $53 million.

A Permanent Court for Atrocities

The ICC institutionalizes the concept of the international tribunal for crimes against humanity. However, the court is not a venue of first resort. Instead, individuals accused of committing a crime against humanity must be tried by their own government, if that government has ratified the treaty. The accused would come before the ICC only if their home country was unable or unwilling to act. In order to prevent malicious or frivolous accusations, the statute requires prosecutors to justify their decisions according to generally recognized principles that would exclude politically motivated charges. The Security Council has the authority to halt an improper prosecution.

Because the US has been a staunch supporter of previous tribunals, we would expect an equally enthusiastic response to the ICC. The Clinton administration signed the treaty in its closing weeks, although with reservations, but the Bush administration stated that it would not send the treaty to Congress for ratification without major changes aimed at protecting US military and government personnel against "politically motivated war crimes prosecutions." The Bush administration substantially hardened its stance, removing the US signature from the treaty, to the delight of congressional conservatives who claim it violates US sovereignty. Friends of the treaty minimize the sovereignty issue by noting that the document includes language for "harmonizing" international law with domestic law.

The White House has declared that the United States government will offer no cooperation with the court and provide no information to its prosecutors. A friend of the treaty, Senator Russell Feingold

(D-Wisc.), questioned the government's sudden about-face, less than two years after the previous president had signed the treaty. Feingold claims that the turnabout may hinder the effort against international terrorism because the United States may find it hard to ask nations to honor international commitments against terror and violence while the United States itself shows "a lack of respect for multilateralism."

The issue is not totally or only the darling of conservatives. Some US journalists worry that international tribunals compromise the objectivity and effectiveness of the press by asking, and in some cases compelling, war correspondents to testify in court against alleged war criminals. Nina Bernstein examined the issue in a 2002 *New York Times* story about an American correspondent, Jonathan Randal, who had reported on the war in the Balkans and been subpoenaed to testify at the International Tribunal for the Former Yugoslavia. Instead of testifying, Randal filed an appeal and won. In a precedent-setting move, the court agreed that he should not be compelled to testify, and further ruled that "to subpoena a war correspondent the evidence sought must be 'of direct and important value in determining a core issue of the case' and cannot be reasonably obtained elsewhere." This decision is the first by any tribunal that offers legal protection to war correspondents, and it will probably be cited by other tribunals and the ICC, according to lawyers Bernstein interviewed for the article. Until the ICC makes a formal statement on the issue, however, the legal status of journalists in the court's proceedings remains ambiguous.

While the White House and Congress have stalled ratification, the rest of the world has been steadily moving toward making the ICC a reality. In March 2003, the court was officially inaugurated in The Hague. Its first chief prosecutor, Argentine lawyer Luis Moreno Ocampo, was elected a month later.

CHAPTER 11

The Call for Reform

*Other than its membership, whom is the UN accountable to? Its member-
ship is of state parties, many of which are authoritarian governments, who
couldn't give a damn what their people think of it. There aren't checks and
balances by public constituencies over what member states do at the UN, so
it's undemocratic in that sense. It's also undemocratic in the sense that it is
dominated by a few key members, particularly the P5, and the power of the
veto.*
—Shepard Forman, New York University's Center on
International Cooperation

The controversy we reviewed in Chapter 5 about "reforming" the
Security Council to make it more relevant to modern times, echoes
throughout the UN. Loud voices from many corners call for reforms,
or at least improvements, in most of the bodies, agencies, and activities that constitute the UN. The calls are fed partly by concern that
the Secretariat, the agencies, and other parts of the UN system could
be much more effective, efficient, and accountable than they are, and
partly by allegations that the bureaucracy has been a juicy career plum
for a small group of administrators who put their interests ahead of

those of the organization. As always with the UN, perception readily passes for reality, and the illusion of change can be just as much a goad to praise or criticism as actual change.

Richard Holbrooke argues that the UN "is the flawed but indispensable institution that we have two choices with: weaken it by undermining it or trying to strengthen it by getting it to correct its flaws." For him, the choice is obvious: "In America when we discern flaws we try to fix them. We should do the same with the UN because in the end, it's a highly leveraged organization that helps America and the nation's interest and world. But what a mess it is." He analyzes internal US politics this way: "The Congress, a critical variable, is divided into three types of people: the group that hates the UN is probably 20 percent; 40 percent supports the UN strongly, [which is] most of the Democrats; then you have the swing vote in the middle, the group that will support the UN if they reform, and that is the group that you need to bring on board. That takes real leadership on the part of the US executive branch as well as support from the UN leadership."

Others complain that the UN response to calls for reform has too often been knee-jerk and has not tried to address the significant problems that exist within the bureaucracy. Forman criticizes the UN for acting in so self-referencing a manner. He begins with the assumption that "it's a membership organization, and that most membership organizations' first order of business is to serve their membership." That is hard to do with such a diverse membership, however, and it places a lot of pressure on the Secretary General to act more as a mediator than a leader. But the ultimate problem, Forman believes, is the lack of accountability. Unlike the US government, the UN doesn't have an effective system of checks and balances.

The accountability issue surfaces also in comments by Michael Sheehan. If the UN is indeed like a membership organization, we would expect power to be decentralized among the members. That ought to encourage executives and staffers to avoid making any decision to which a member might take exception. Sheehan complains that at the UN this tendency is evident, as some staff try to "push decision-making upward." "Recommendations made are buried in

Talent Wrapped in Red Tape

"I do want to debunk the notion that the UN has nothing but dead wood. That is completely wrong. The UN has a number of very good people. But the UN is bound up in rules, most of them imposed by the member states. The red tape at the UN is, I don't need to tell you, completely dysfunctional."   —David Malone

nuance in page 3 of a memo. No one takes a stand. And that's what grinds down this bureaucracy, this lack of clarity in options, lack of clarity in decision-making, kick decisions upstairs and then micro-managing." He sees a reluctance to make decisions and take risks, although he admits that "since I've been here I've been supported by those who've asked me to come here and work."

The UN's Response

One of the first substantive efforts by the UN to address the criticisms came in 1994 with the establishment of the Office of Internal Oversight Services (OIOS), charged with making the bureaucracy more effective and efficient. Creation of the office thrilled the US government, which described it as "one of the most significant management reforms adopted by the General Assembly in many years."

When Kofi Annan took office in 1997, he launched what he called his "quiet revolution," to streamline the organization and make it both more efficient and more effective without raising costs. The quiet revolution managed to stop the Secretariat's budget creep for a few years, beginning in 1998, and even reduced it a little. Although the UN claims that the total number of all staff in the UN system (about 52,000) is much smaller than the number of employees at many large corporations, it has nevertheless tried to keep the number from growing too fast. The Secretariat's staff fell from about 12,000 in 1984–85 to 8,900. The Secretariat gained a new reform tool in December

2000, when the General Assembly authorized it to start "results-based budgeting." Long urged by the US as a way of rationalizing the allocation and spending of funds, results-based budgeting establishes objectives for each department or program and develops "performance indicators" to measure progress in reaching them.

Most observers credit Annan's quiet revolution with making real improvements. Madeleine Albright remembers that when she became UN Rep, she was told that "the UN was too bureaucratic to change, and too big ever to achieve consensus on measures to improve its governance." She gleefully counters, "Those cynics were wrong. We have made impressive progress. UN headquarters and the entire UN system are better led than they have ever been. UN leaders and members can take pride in the gains made, but we all know there is much more work to be done." Nancy Soderberg rates the Secretariat as "a collection of really dynamic individuals who care deeply about the organization and really work their tails off, interspersed with incompetent people who are there for regional balance, who are just never going to get fired."

One of the most objective and carefully reasoned analyses of reform came in May 2000, after the US Congress asked its research arm, the General Accounting Office, to do an evaluation. The report was generally positive, much to everyone's surprise. It praised the restructuring of the UN's leadership and operations but warned that the main reform objectives had not yet been achieved, particularly the goal of holding the Secretariat accountable for "accomplishing missions" rather than merely "carrying out activities." The main barrier to change was the General Assembly, which insisted on passing excessive numbers of resolutions for the Secretariat to carry out. In the most recent two-year period, the GA had more than doubled the number of its resolutions, and fully one-fifth of them "had vague or open-ended expectations." The report further noted that while coordination among agencies in the field had improved, much remained to be done in that regard. Richard Holbrooke is blunter: "The field coordination is appalling, and the agencies in the field have no real single head. They have a coordinator system that doesn't work."

UNESCO

One agency in particular has demonstrated both the need for reform at the UN and the ability of a committed executive to make reform a reality. The US is a founding member of UNESCO, the UN Educational, Scientific, and Cultural Organization, but in 1984 withdrew from full membership (and payment of annual dues), citing as its reasons alleged politicization and mismanagement. During succeeding years, rumors persisted not only in the US but elsewhere that the organization was poorly run, and some observers claimed that it was losing its institutional focus and momentum. It was charged, for example, that UNESCO's important office in Brasilia could not account for a large portion of its funds. Things came to a head in 1999, when a leaked internal UNESCO document described favoritism, nepotism, corruption, and poor management throughout the organization. The Canadian government was so concerned that it conducted its own investigation, which largely confirmed the charges. Media coverage in the US and abroad gave the organization bad publicity and seemed to vindicate those US critics of UNESCO who had encouraged the American pullout fifteen years before. The very existence of the organization seemed to be at stake.

Change came with the election in 2000 of a new director, Koichiro Matsuura, who had been Japan's ambassador to France. After moving quickly to slash the number of field offices and upper-level administrators and make other cuts in staff and costs, he addressed the agency's accountability problem by proposing creation of a single internal oversight system that would replace an array of audit and evaluation departments and units. This reform began with an impartial investigation by a team from a private organization, the Institute of Internal Auditors, who in summer 2000 did a business-focused quality assurance review of the agency's auditing, evaluation, and investigative functions. Their draft report, presented in September 2000 (and available on UNESCO's website), mentioned, among other points, that "the current internal monitoring functions of UNESCO generally do not conform to the *Standards for the Professional Practice of*

Internal Auditing, which is a widely used approach for structuring an organization's mechanism of internal financial and management controls. Their proposed changes would bring UNESCO into harmony with this standard and give it new tools for managing its projects and funds.

The team's report provided a basis for implementing the kind of far-reaching changes that the director had been seeking. UNESCO's Executive Board approved the creation of a consolidated internal oversight system in September 2000. One of the new office's first assignments was to investigate the mismanagement allegations at the Brasilia office. It found "weaknesses in the control environment," while an external auditing group found problems that "were serious" and might call in question UNESCO's financial statements for the 2000–2001 fiscal year.

It is clear that Director Matsuura is pushing hard to give the organization a squeaky-clean look. Additionally, he has been refocusing the organization on issues of growing global importance, and has done it in such a way as to attract favorable US interest. One of UNESCO's projects, for example, involved reopening schools in Afghanistan after the US-led overthrow of the Taliban; another was to help preserve Iraq's cultural heritage after the US-led invasion against the regime of Saddam Hussein. In 2002, President Bush declared that the US would soon rejoin UNESCO, and subsequently Congress approved payment of American dues to the organization. In only a few years, the organization experienced a complete turnaround in its image and relationship with the US government.

An obvious way of reforming the UN would be to choose strong directors for the various agencies. If UNESCO has finally obtained an effective and reform-minded director, why not go the same route for all the other agencies, programs, and commissions? It is a reasonable thought that turns out to be difficult to implement. Some UN insiders have suggested that because running a nation requires many skills, former heads of government would make good UN directors. David Malone regards this "strange belief" as naïve. "UN agencies are much harder to run than governments, particularly in the western world,"

Answers to Common Questions

Understandably, most Americans know little about the inner workings of the UN administration and are therefore likely to take at face value complaints about excessively good pay and benefits and special perks like free parking. The following items, adapted from the UN's website, give the other side of the argument. Note, however, that they refer mainly to the Secretariat in New York City, not to the specialized agencies, which have their own procedures and pay scales.

STAFF SELECTION

To complaints that the UN hires by quota more than by merit, the UN replies that the Charter requires the Secretariat to be sure its staff reflects "the whole membership of the UN, so that it will be responsive to the diverse political, social and cultural systems in the world and so that all Member States will have confidence in it. To ensure such diversity, the UN employs qualified people from all over the world, and recruits globally. Tough competitive examinations are used to recruit the core professional staff at the junior and middle levels." In any case, nationals of developing countries compose only 44 percent of the "core" professional posts at the UN.

COMPENSATION

The UN bases its professional salaries "on a direct, net comparison with the pay of United States federal civil service employees, adjusted to reflect differences in cost-of-living expenses between New York City and Washington, D.C." If anything, says the UN, its pay is on the low side and is often a hindrance to recruiting the best people.

The UN operates on an internal merit system. "The pay of United Nations staff is regulated by the International Civil Service Commission, an independent, 15-member body of experts representing all regions of the world. The Commission reports to the United Nations General Assembly."

UN staff are not supposed to double-dip. "UN employees are not permitted, under staff regulations, to accept supplementary payments or subsidies from their Governments, in order not to compromise their independence as international civil servants."

The head of the UN, the Secretary General, receives an annual salary of about $227,000, which is "far below that of the chief executives of many businesses."

All UN staff pay income tax. A "staff assessment" is deducted from their gross salary at the rate of 30 to 34 percent, with no deductions allowed, so it is effectively a "flat tax." US citizens working for the UN pay the US Social Security tax. "UN employees (except for the very few with diplomatic status) pay the same sales, real estate and other taxes as anyone else."

BENEFITS AND PERKS

Most UN staff have no diplomatic status or other special standing, and must obey all local laws. Approximately 120 UN employees, including the Secretary General and the most senior officials of the UN system, have diplomatic status.

Diplomats (as distinct from staff) do not work for the UN but for their own governments. "All Member States maintain in New York 'permanent missions,' which in effect are their countries' embassies to the UN. Missions are headed by ambassadors, known as permanent representatives, who make up the core of the diplomatic community in New York."

And finally, there is no free parking. Employees must pay to park in the on-premises UN garage, "which has limited space."

he asserts. Whereas western democracies "pretty much run themselves," and the prime minister simply makes policy, UN agencies "are very resistant to direction from the top on policy even more than on administrative reform and are a much bigger challenge for a head."

Malone cites the case of Ruud Lubbers, one of the most successful prime ministers in recent Dutch history, who "presided over coalitions that were unstable that he held together, that brought about an economic miracle in the Netherlands—a highly successful guy." The Office of the UN High Commissioner for Refugees, however, may be more of a challenge. "The administrative problems of UNHCR, which he's tackled very bravely, are resisting the types of solutions he's proposing. Refugee problems of a very fundamental nature keep arising that aren't susceptible to the easy solutions that are often possible in government. How do you deal with Australia when it turns back refugees from Afghanistan on a ship, knowing Australia is the country that takes the most refugees per capita in the world other than Canada? Lubbers has to stand up for refugees, but Australians by and large do a fabulous job on refugees. So he doesn't want to completely alienate Australia."

Perhaps the final word on the reform question should go to Richard Holbrooke, who cautions against harping excessively on the bureaucracy's failings. "We've got to be very careful as Americans not to be holier than thou because we have an inefficient bureaucracy as well, and ours is much larger and better funded." Amen.

CHAPTER 12

UN Finances

With throats parched by a week of talks on the Middle East, U.N. Security Council members carried their own mineral water to meetings after the United Nations cut the budget for pitchers of iced tap water. A plan to balance the world body's $2.625 billion two-year administrative budget calls for about $75 million in cuts—including lowering heat, rationing air conditioning and eliminating pitchers and glasses of ice water at meetings.

—Reuters, Apr. 8, 2002

How the UN gets and manages its funds has been under fire, from critics both outside and inside the system. The debate about getting funds has focused on three big issues. First is the long-standing problem of US arrears to the UN (a matter largely settled, at least for now) and how much the organization's largest patron should pay. Second is how the UN can operate with less waste and more efficiency. And third is whether it is legitimate to expand the variety of income sources through relationships with the corporate world. These issues raise sensitive questions. If the United States pays less, doesn't everyone else have to pay more? Could the search for corporate-related income risk new dangers such as "selling out" to big business?

Many Budgets

Debates about UN finances require distinguishing among the major budgets of the world body. Most discussions in the media relate to the "regular budget," which pays for activities, staff, and basic infrastructure but not peacekeeping. In 2002, this was $1.149 billion. (The regular budget is for a two-year period, a biennium, so $1.149 is simply half of the $2.29 billion that the General Assembly approved when it voted on the budget.) Peacekeeping expenses are treated separately. Annual peacekeeping costs peaked at $3.5 billion in 1994, during the large-scale operations in the former Yugoslavia, dropped to $1.3 billion in 1997, and rose toward the $3 billion level in 2002. It is estimated that the total cost for the regular budget, peacekeeping, the UN agencies, funds, and programs, excluding the World Bank and the IMF, comes to some $11 billion each year.

Behind these big and round numbers lie the complexities that give the UN its unique flavor. When asked about the size of his agency's budget, Mark Malloch Brown of the United Nations Development Program (UNDP) replied: "I call it $1.2 billion, and there are two other numbers which others use. One is $750 million, which is core contributions. I call it $1.2 billion because that's core plus donor contributions to special trust funds for special issues. Some call it $2 billion because that includes what we call co-financing, where developed countries kick in a huge volume of resources because they like us, in many cases, to spend their money for them. I count that out because for various reasons not dealt with it's a little misleading. So I say $1.2 billion, pessimists say $750 million, the optimists say $2 billion or $2.1. And it's growing. Last year the core in dollar terms grew 4%." Is that perfectly clear?

As the UN constantly points out, its budgets are pretty small potatoes in today's world of trillion-dollar economies. For example, the UN's website notes that "the budget for UN worldwide human rights activities is smaller than that of the Zürich Opera House." And again: "The budget of the World Health Organization is equivalent to that of a medium-sized teaching hospital in an industrial country."

UN Budget 2002

Regular: $1.149 billion
Peacekeeping: $2.77 billion (July 2001–June 2002)

Money Talks

"The test of the American commitment to the UN, above all, is financial. That's what tests it, and whether we seek to strengthen the UN
through a combination of resources and reform or weaken it through
neglect and punishment. On that point this administration appears
to be conflicted internally. I have no doubt at all Colin Powell wants to
strengthen the UN, but it is not clear whether other members of the
administration share that view."   —Richard Holbrooke

Remarkably, the budgets have not increased appreciably during the
past decade. In fact, when adjusted for inflation and currency fluctua-
tions, the UN regular budget declined during several years, so that for
1998–99 it was actually 3 percent less than in 1996–97.

Sources of Income

The income to support the regular budget comes from assessments of
member states. Membership in the UN comes with the obligation to
help pay for its support—something that has never been questioned.
Instead, the focus has been on the size of the contribution a state has
to make. The formula for contributing is based largely on the nation's
share of the world economy. In other words, the rich pay more than
the poor. The United States, having the world's largest economy by a
wide margin, naturally pays the largest share, and very poor nations
pay a nominal amount.

Strictly speaking, the contributions don't follow economic size. For

What's a Few Billion among Friends?

"The remarkable thing about China and Russia, both of which nowadays have virtually no interest in most of the developing world, is that they have not sought to block rather expensive peacekeeping operations serving the interests of Africa or Eastern Europe. In that way the Russians and the Chinese are rather different from Americans. . . . Russia went to great lengths to pay its arrears to the UN. It knows that the US will always quibble over dollars and cents, so it leaves the dirty work to the US."   —David Malone

example, the Vatican, which ranks as an affluent organization, pays only $2,776 a year for its observer status (2002), which carries no vote but enables it to wield great influence in debates and meetings. Far poorer nations have to pay a minimum of about $11,104 annually for their UN dues (which, admittedly, includes the right to vote in the GA).

A few of the rich states have actually sought to get their assessments reduced. The United States has negotiated several reductions in its share of the general budget. For example, in 1974 the UN agreed to place a cap of 25 percent on the size of a member state's assessment, effectively lowering the United States' share in subsequent years. Another change came in 2000, when the General Assembly reduced the US share of the regular budget to a maximum of 22 percent, and its share of peacekeeping costs from 31 percent to about 27 percent. Both reductions came at the urging of the US government, based on the Helms-Biden Law, which stipulated that the US would pay nearly $1 billion in arrears over three years if the UN met certain conditions, such as a reduction in the assessment rate. Congress praised the rate reduction of 2001, and so did many others both at the UN and abroad, who felt that a major bone of contention between the US and the UN had finally been removed.

However, other nations were less enchanted with this reduction

Table 2 Fifteen Most Highly Assessed Member States for Regular Budget,
2002 (Total: $1.149 billion)

Country	Assessment in $ millions	% Share of UN General Budget
United States	$283.0	22.00%
Japan	218.4	19.67
Germany	109.3	9.9
France	72.3	6.5
United Kingdom	61.9	5.6
Italy	56.6	5.1
Canada	28.6	2.5
Spain	28.1	2.5
Brazil	23.2	2.1
South Korea	20.7	1.9
Netherlands	19.4	1.8
Australia	18.2	1.6
China	17.1	1.6
Russia	13.3	1.2
Argentina	12.8	1.2
Totals	$982.9	85.2%

Source: www.un.org

because they assumed that they were being asked to pick up the slack.
To its credit, the US government responded to complaints. The State
Department, in its annual report about the UN in 2000, announced
that the US government had taken the unprecedented act of offering
"to compensate countries in year 2001 in order to mitigate the impact
of the reduction in ceiling rate from 25 to 22 percent." This meant that
ninety-one countries would be spared raises in their assessment for
one year. The compensation was the result of a gift from the Turner
Foundation to the US State Department, which passed on the funds to
the UN.

Despite the adjustment, the US and several other large developed
nations remain major funders of the UN, contributing some 85 percent of the regular budget, as Table 2 shows.

Peacekeeping is treated separately from other budgets. The scale used to make peacekeeping assessments has ten levels of support, with the least developed countries paying 10 percent of what they would have owed according to the assessment scale for the regular budget and the five permanent Security Council members paying a surcharge of about 25 percent. In 2001, the US share of peacekeeping costs was reduced from 31 percent to about 27 percent.

Ideally, each member state accepts its assessment as being appropriate and immediately sends a check to the UN for the full amount. Reality is more complicated. Even for routine and predictable budgets, like the regular budget, the UN has a hard time getting everyone to pay fully and on time. By May 31, 2002, for example, only 80 members, some 40 percent of the membership, had paid their 2002 dues, leaving the UN having to wait for 110 countries. Many of the poor nations cannot afford to pay their full assessment and are in arrears. Still others have delayed their payments for various reasons, usually unrelated to their ability to pay. The Charter (Article 19) permits the UN to penalize a member that is two years in arrears by taking away its vote in the GA. This has been done quite a bit, as a last resort, and even the US has found itself in danger of penalization during years when it was withholding its dues or paying them slowly to express its unhappiness with the UN.

Fairness

A complaint, not specific to the United States, is that the many small nations can control the regular budget through their voting power in the General Assembly. The United States has long complained about being outvoted by blocs of members, such as the Group of 77 (a coalition of UN member states from Third World countries), and having little effective control over how the UN spends its money. The UN's general budget is the product of a complicated process designed to ensure that all interested parties have their say in how funds are obtained and spent. The Secretary General proposes a draft budget and gives it to the Advisory Committee on Administrative and Budgetary Questions (ACABQ) for review. The committee consists of sixteen

From the UN Charter, Chapter IV: The General Assembly

ARTICLE 19

A Member of the United Nations which is in arrears in the payment of its financial contributions to the Organization shall have no vote in the General Assembly if the amount of its arrears equals or exceeds the amount of the contributions due from it for the preceding two full years. The General Assembly may, nevertheless, permit such a Member to vote if it is satisfied that the failure to pay is due to conditions beyond the control of the Member.

In May 2002, 21 member states were without their vote in the General Assembly under Article 19:

Afghanistan	Kyrgyzstan
Burundi*	Liberia
Central African Republic	Mauritania
Chad	Republic of Moldova
Comoros*	Sao Tome and Principe
Democratic Republic of the Congo	Seychelles
Dominica	Somalia
Georgia	Tajikistan
Niger	Uzbekistan
Guinea-Bissau	Vanuatu
Iraq	

*The General Assembly, citing extenuating circumstances, permitted these countries to exercise their vote until June 30, 2002.

individuals nominated by their governments, usually including a US national, and elected by the General Assembly. The Committee for Program and Coordination, made up of thirty-four experts elected by the General Assembly, reviews the program aspects of the budget. Unlike the Advisory Committee, in which the experts serve in their personal capacity, the Program Committee experts represent the

Secretary General Kofi Annan meets with members of the US Senate Foreign Relations Committee on Jan. 21, 2000. Attending are US Ambassador
Richard Holbrooke (second on left); Committee Chairman and Senator
Jesse Helms (third on left), and ranking Democratic Senator Joseph Biden
(fourth on left). UN/DPI photo by Evan Schneider.

views of their governments. The revised draft is sent to the General
Assembly for approval, when it becomes the official UN general budget for the next biennium. Each country has the opportunity to suggest changes in the draft budget, but the changes may not necessarily
be adopted.

The UN replies to criticisms from affluent nations that a lot of the
money it spends eventually finds its way back to the major donors. For
example, the UN's headquarters is in New York City, where UN staff
and diplomats contribute to the city's economy. Additionally, developed countries supply a substantial share of UN employees and consultants. US citizens make up the greatest single national share of
Secretariat employees (not surprising, given that the Secretariat is in
New York City).

But other statistics tell a different story, according to a study just

Helms-Biden Law

The Helms-Biden Law put the US on course to pay nearly $1 billion in back dues over three years, providing the UN met certain benchmarks:

Year 1: Conditions were met: US paid $100 million toward arrears in 1999.
Year 2: UN agreed to new assessment rates for regular budget and peacekeeping:
US paid $582 million in 2001.
Year 3: US paid $244 million.

completed by the US General Accounting Office (GAO). It seems that both Japan and the United States are underrepresented among staff at the UN in relation to their financial contributions to the world body, while British, French, and Canadian citizens are overrepresented. The GAO examined the Secretariat and six agencies that had established hiring quotas, concluding that only the Secretariat met its own goals for hiring US citizens. Similarly, Japan, despite contributing 19.5 percent of the UN budget, held only 2 percent of senior positions, while twelve countries, including Russia, the Philippines, and Pakistan, were overrepresented in the Secretariat.

The US State Department came up with similar conclusions when it did its own estimate of national representation. It examined hiring patterns in the Secretariat and four agencies that have established a system of "described ranges," or quotas: the Food and Agriculture Organization (FAO), International Civil Aviation Organization (ICAO), International Labor Organization (ILO), and World Health Organization (WHO). Table 3 lists the Secretariat and the agencies, along with the number and status of Americans on board as of December 2000. (These figures represent only the professional posts funded from the agencies' assessed budgets.)

At first glance the hiring pattern seems clearly discriminatory

Table 3 Number and Status of US Nationals in the UN Secretariat and
Selected Agencies, as of December 2000

UN Agency	Filled	US Desirable Range or Quota	Number of Americans on Board	Percent of Americans on Board	Current Status
UN	2,400	314–424	315	13.1	In range
FAO	992	186–248	126	12.7	Underrepresented
ICAO	221	28	16	7.2	Underrepresented
ILO	659	101–135	87	13.2	Underrepresented
WHO	1,138	174–237	152	13.4	Underrepresented

Source: State Department, USParticipation in the UN, 2000, p. 125.

against the US. However, the report explains that the failure of the US
to pay its dues on time, and in some cases to pay its contributions to
specific agencies either on time or at all, caused a realignment of
hiring patterns in favor of other donor nations. The case for "discrimination" is therefore unclear.

Additional Funding

Not all UN funding comes directly from member states. UNICEF
holiday cards, for example, have long provided additional income for
efforts to aid children. In addition, UN agencies and organizations
sometimes receive grants from foundations, such as the Turner Foundation or the Bill & Melinda Gates Foundation. Recently, however, a
new line of fiscal opportunity has opened up with the creation of
partnerships between the UN and large businesses.

The appeal is obvious. By tapping corporate support the UN can
possibly avoid having to raise the amounts that member states pay,
thus sidestepping the contentious issues associated with who pays
how much, and how funds should be spent. A danger is also evident:
the appearance of undue business influence in the affairs of an organization that is supposed to act disinterestedly.

The overture to the corporate world has alarmed some observers as a potential sellout to business interests. An early outcry came when it was learned that one UN agency had asked sixteen large transnational corporations for donations of $50,000 each to pay for a Global Sustainable Development Facility. The UNDP was criticized by international watchdog groups for selling out to corporate interests, a charge the agency strongly denied. Rather, the agency claimed it was seeking to demonstrate that corporations can be both profitable and good citizens.

Shepard Forman has offered his own, tongue-in-cheek solution for the UN's funding problems. "I once suggested rather facetiously that there should be a reverse scale of assessments in which countries that act badly and therefore cost the UN more to patch things up than to fix things up should have to pay more dues. There should be a system where if you misbehave very badly your membership should be suspended or something else occurs. Otherwise anybody can do what they want, they can get away with anything they want, and the membership doesn't live up to the organization's own set of standards."

CHAPTER 13

A Tour of UN Headquarters

*In many ways [the UN is] a direct throwback to the '50s. The building itself
is a throwback to the '50s with [period] chairs and everything, and there are
still a lot of people that are stuck with the . . . mentality of North vs South,
blaming the US for all their evils.*

—Nancy Soderberg, former US Ambassador to the United Nations

Nancy Soderberg's quip has a kernel of truth, in that walking
through the UN headquarters complex in New York City can feel like
being in a museum. Never having enjoyed or endured a major renovation, the building and its furnishings are pretty much as they were
when opened to the public during the early 1950s. As for her complaint about old ways of thinking, we can't blame that on the architec-
ture, which has retained its freshness and still delights any eye that
can overlook the worn fittings, cracked plaster, and peeling paint. The
UN's leadership must find a way of maintaining the buildings while
also making them better work spaces, and they must do that soon if
the structures are to remain safe for both tenants and the thousands of
visitors and tourists. The UN has cut its operating budget so much
that it can't do proper maintenance, let alone renovate. There's too
little heat in winter and not enough air conditioning in summer.

The United Nations headquarters in Manhattan.
UN photo 165054 by Lois Conner.

Despite its signs of wear and tear, the UN complex remains a popular tourist attraction. Opposite the complex, stretching from 48th Street and First Avenue to 42nd Street, is a long line of flagpoles—191 of them—each bearing the flag of a UN member state. The flags are arranged alphabetically, with Afghanistan starting at 48th Street and Zimbabwe finishing at 42nd Street. The line nicely frames the UN complex, like a grand boulevard.

Immediately beyond the flags, the blue-green glass slab of the Secretariat building, which houses UN staff, is so instantly recognizable and well placed in the complex that it seems to grow organically from the soil. It was designed by an international team of architects who adapted a concept of the French architect Le Corbusier. John D. Rocke-

Flags of UN member states fly at the UN headquarters. UN photo 185522 by A. Brizzi.

feller Jr. donated the eighteen-acre UN Headquarters site, which was
cleared of its structures in 1947. The thirty-nine-storey Secretariat
building was finished in 1950, and on the thirty-eighth floor are the
UN Secretary General's offices.

Before entering through the glass doors to the visitors reception hall
in the General Assembly building with its central information booth,
visitors pass through UN security, located in a large tent erected after
September 11 to provide an expanded checkpoint at the UN's visitor's
entrance. The complex draws tourists and schoolchildren, as well as
members of the media and consultants who have business related to
the UN. Since 9/11, the UN security force is more visible and active
than ever before. So, although the security tent has ruined the view of

A stained glass memorial designed by Russian-born French artist Marc
Chagall in memory of Dag Hammarskjöld. UN photo by Lois Connor.

the building façade, this seems a small price to pay for prudence. In
addition to the security force, the UN operates its own postal administration (UN postage stamps are available only in the complex) and
fire department.

Exhibition spaces are located in the eastern portion of the complex.
Exhibits include artworks from a permanent collection and traveling
shows such as children's art from around the world. One of the most
eye-catching artistic features in the complex is a stained glass window
by Marc Chagall, a gift from the artist and United Nations staff members. It was presented in memory of Secretary General Dag Hammarskjöld and fifteen others who died in a plane crash in 1961. Among the
many paintings that hang on the walls are objects displayed in cases.
Ironically, though, no maps are displayed. You would think a global
organization would obsess on maps, but it turns out they're too politically sensitive. In the General Assembly Hall, discussed below, is a
map of the world—without national boundaries drawn. Here it's the

art that has been subjected to political correctness: none has been donated by any member nation; instead the walls feature two abstract murals by Fernand Leger, donated anonymously through the United Nations Association of the USA.

The complex consists of four large, interconnected buildings: the General Assembly Building, the Conference Building, the Secretariat building, and the Dag Hammarskjöld Library. In the basement of the General Assembly Building, visitors will find restrooms, a book and gift shop, and a post office.

Guided tours of the complex start in the General Assembly Building, which is the site of the General Assembly Hall. The hall is open to the public when the assembly is not in session. It's the largest room in the complex, seating more than 1,800. The delegates sit in alphabetical order, according to lots drawn before each annual session. Certainly this is a space made for speaking, although a former US Ambassador here, Richard Holbrooke, always complained about its having bad acoustics. Delegates have earphones that provide them with simultaneous translations into Arabic, Chinese, French, Russian, Spanish, or English.

Next on the tour is the Conference Building, which includes the chambers of the Security Council, the Trusteeship Council, and the Economic and Social Council, all lined up in a row. The Security Council Chamber is a clean and workable space, a gift from Norway designed by architect Arnstein Arneberg. The main room features the famous horseshoe table where the delegates confer during the "formals," the public sessions. A small side room is for the "informals." The decoration here is inspirational—a big canvas depicting a phoenix rising from the ashes, and a blue and gold silk tapestry. The images on the drapes of the windows overlooking the East River symbolize faith, charity, and hope.

The Economic and Social Council Chamber, a gift from Sweden, was designed by Sven Markelius, one of the original architects of the complex. The ductwork in the ceiling was left exposed as a reminder that the UN's economic and social work is never finished.

One of the least known and most interesting rooms in the complex

The UN is one of New York City's most popular sites to visit, drawing about 400,000 visitors every year. Since 1952, some 37 million visitors have taken a tour.

If You Go

You might consider first orienting yourself by taking the UN's online tour, *http://www.un.org/Overview/Tours/UNHQ/*
   Guided tours of the UN operate daily from the General Assembly Public Lobby and take visitors to some of the main council chambers and the General Assembly Hall. In the public concourse, downstairs, the Public Inquiries Unit offers additional information materials relating to the UN and its agencies. Also in the concourse is the United Nations postal counter (which sells UN stamps), along with a UN bookstore, gift shops, coffee shop, and restrooms.

HOURS

January and February: Monday–Friday, 9:30 am–4:45 pm
The rest of the year: 7 days a week, 9:30 am–4:45 pm
May is usually the busiest month. English tours leave every half hour and last for about one hour.
   The UN is closed on Thanksgiving Day, Christmas Day, and New Year's Day. A limited schedule may be in effect during the general debate of the GA (mid-September to mid-October), between Christmas and New Year, and during special conferences and events.

DIRECTIONS

The UN Headquarters is on First Avenue between 42nd Street and 48th Streets. The visitor's entrance is located on First Avenue at 46th Street. The UN does not offer public parking.
Subway: 4, 5, 6, or 7 line to Grand Central Terminal, then walk 42nd St. to First Ave.
Buses: M15, M27, M42, or M104

TOUR PRICES

Adults: $10.00
Senior citizens: $8.50
Students: $6.50
Children* (ages 5–14): $5.50
*Note that children under 5 are not admitted.

RESERVATIONS AND GROUPS

Reservations are required for 12 or more people and should be made by calling 212–963–4440, faxing 212–963–0071, or emailing *unitg@UN.org*

A complimentary ticket is issued for the first 15 tickets purchased and one free one for every 20 tickets thereafter.

CONTACT INFO

General info: 212–963-TOUR
Languages other than English: 212–963–7539
Group reservations: 212–963–4440

LANGUAGES

Tours are conducted in the following languages: English, Arabic, Croatian, Danish, French, German, Greek, Hebrew, Italian, Japanese, Korean, Mandarin, Polish, Portuguese, Russian, Spanish, Swedish. Call to be sure a tour in your language is available the day you plan to visit.

HANDICAP ACCESS

The UN is accessible to people with disabilities and provides wheel-chairs for those visitors who require them. People with hearing dis-abilities may obtain written information on the tour.

is the Trusteeship Council Chamber. A gift from Denmark, it was designed by the Danish architect Finn Juhl. The acoustics are reportedly excellent, but this hardly matters because the Trusteeship Council no longer meets. This room, designed for what was once a major part of the UN, has fallen silent because its main tenant is no longer relevant to the functioning of the UN. Delegates no longer sit around the table here, gazing at the large wooden statue of a woman with her arms outstretched and releasing a bird. The sculpture, donated in 1953, when the UN still had trust territories (islands and lands lacking self-government), is carved from teak, a wood associated with some of those territories.

The final building in the complex is the Dag Hammarskjöld Library. The building was a gift from the Ford Foundation (whose headquarters is down the street, on 42nd Street). Although its collections are available to the public, the library is used mostly by UN staff and diplomats. As you might guess, the library includes vast stores of information about the UN.

The staff cafeteria is one part of the UN that has definitely improved over the years; the food is better and in greater variety. Best of all is the view, overlooking the East River through huge windows. The cafeteria isn't open to the general public, but, oddly enough, the Delegates' Dining Room is. Rated a "NY secret treasure" by the *Zagat Survey of New York City Restaurants,* the dining room is on the fourth floor and is open to the public for lunch, featuring a "diverse selection of international cuisine." It too offers a view of the East River. According to Richard Holbrooke, food is what holds the UN together.

Delegates have two lounges in which to relax. Both are located in the Conference Building and are very popular sites for delegates to sit with one another after a meeting adjourns to talk over negotiations or details of a meeting, or just socialize. These lounges could be considered the "informal" chambers of the different councils, where horse-trading takes place. Of course, no lounge would be complete without a huge rug depicting the Great Wall of China, a gift from the Republic of China. On upper floors are the tiny offices of the journalists and other media people who report on the UN. And of course, the UN personnel are there too.

Several schemes have been floated to pay for renovating the complex, but none of them has gone anywhere yet. Recently, Kofi Annan asked the US State Department to consider making a $1 billion interest-free loan to the UN, to pay for renovation of the complex and construction of an additional building to house UN agencies. By stretching out repayment to twenty-five or thirty years, it would be possible for the UN to repay the loan without straining its budget. There is another way to go, but no one seems willing to consider it. The UN doesn't have to be located in New York City. It could move, if another nation offered it a more economical deal. Just as sports franchises move from city to city in search of the best domed stadium, the UN could shop around for the best offer. A few years ago a media report claimed the German government was interested in providing the UN with space in Bonn vacated by government offices moving to Berlin. Was this a serious offer? Would the members of the UN ever consider leaving New York and all it has to offer? The future will tell.

CHAPTER 14

The Coup Against Boutros-Ghali

Every country probably trashed us. I guess they didn't like the way we did it, but there was no other way. We tried to do it more subtly, we tried to ask Boutros to step down. He had promised he was a one-term, and he reneged on that promise. It got uglier and uglier, so we finally decided to stick to our guns.   —Michael Sheehan

If you think the US government is at the mercy of the UN, or that the UN can dictate policy to the United States, consider the case of Boutros Boutros-Ghali, who was Kofi Annan's predecessor as Secretary General. Boutros-Ghali served one term as SG and declared his intention to run for another. But he never made it, because, to put it bluntly, he fell afoul of key US diplomats and political leaders, who blocked him through a carefully staged coup. The coup is no secret. Boutros-Ghali has described his experiences in writing, and many participants and observers have offered their own contributions. The story merits a brief retelling as an example of the fine line that the SG has to walk in threading a path to successful leadership.

Boutros-Ghali's downfall had two main roots. One of them was the disaffection of his middle managers, who did not lift a finger to defend him when the Americans and their accomplices made their move. Mark Malloch Brown blames Boutros-Ghali's background as a senior official in the Egyptian government for giving him an exalted view of his office, which was exactly the wrong thing to emulate as Secretary General. Instead of making himself indispensable by helping nations solve problems, too many saw him as doing "the diplomatic equivalent of stamping his foot while simultaneously staring down his nose. It didn't make most heads of state and foreign ministers particularly want to work with him."

A highly placed UN insider confirms this picture of an arrogant, isolated Secretary General. "The thing about Boutros that we were most unhappy about as staff was he didn't really like the institution that he headed. He was completely aloof and detached from all of us." His bullying caused the staff to either remain silent or tell him what he wanted to hear, which meant "he was no longer getting the best opinions from people." His manner of working, says the insider, "was hopeless." He would leave managers out of the loop, presenting them with constant administrative and policy surprises. They would often find an ambassador or minister coming to them and saying, "As your boss said the other day" or "As we said to your boss the other day," and they hadn't even been given a copy of the notes on the meeting. "That was really bad for efficiency and for morale."

The Secretariat's staff had to endure these indignities, but not the United States. Once Boutros-Ghali got on the bad side of US Permanent Representative Madeleine Albright, it was all downhill. "Personal dislike was a real issue on policy," says the insider. "In the case of Boutros and Madeleine, he didn't like her style, she didn't like his nature, and their dislike coincided with the fact that professionally they didn't see eye to eye."

Early in 1996 Albright became leader of an American effort to prevent Boutros-Ghali from seeking a second term. It was a period of strained relations between the UN and the US, owing to a string of failed operations (fighting in Somalia and genocidal massacres in Rwanda and Srebrenica). Michael Sheehan, who was on the National Security Council staff at the time, recalls that he found him-

Secretary General Boutros Boutros-Ghali greets President Clinton prior to the president's address before the General Assembly on Sept. 24, 1996. UN/DPI photo by Evan Schneider.

self one of the initial conspirators. "We got together and said Boutros needs to go, he is not good for the UN, and he's not good for the US, and not good for the US and the UN."

The conspirators quickly discovered that while Boutros-Ghali had little solid support in the UN, they had greatly underestimated his determination to run for a second term and his skill in marshalling support. He used "every trick he knew, with very subtle and not so subtle promises and threats to countries. No one wanted to oppose him." "We ended up standing alone in broad daylight," reflects Sheehan, "instead of slipping it to him." The deed would have to be done very publicly, in the modern-day equivalent of the Roman forum.

The conspirators acted with growing support from President Clinton and Secretary of State Warren Christopher, who were put off by Boutros-Ghali's lobbying of member states. "They recognized that he

forgot what his job was," Sheehan says. "He was a servant of the
member states, a servant for the organization not an entity unto himself." Realizing that they needed to have an appealing alternative candidate, the coup team wrote a memo to Clinton in spring 1996 that
offered three candidates—Lakhdar Brahimi, Olara Otunnu, and Kofi
Annan—each of whom was from Africa. Sheehan favored Annan or
Brahimi. "I had been working for both of them and I loved both of
them. At the time I didn't know Otunnu, who was being pushed by
another member of the NSC staff. The President approved this strategy and said that, yes, he needs to go, that sounds good. We also
discussed the Asian option and others, but we thought the post was
going to stay in Africa."

When the Americans began looking for votes in the General Assembly, they discovered that Annan seemed to have the strongest
support, so he became the lead candidate. "The French extracted a
promise from us to support them to get the Under Secretary for
Peacekeeping, which we granted, and they have now. And that was the
deal. Kofi Annan became SG to the delight of everyone." Actually,
much of the "delight" was after the fact. Sheehan recalls that after the
vote, mass amnesia struck and "it was like rats off a sinking ship."
"Now everyone supported Annan from day one, so he was the choice.
I remember differently. We were under enormous pressure to cut a
deal, particularly from [French president] Chirac and [South Africa's]
Nelson Mandela, who called the president on many occasions to lobby
for Boutros-Ghali. I never felt more pressure from anything I ever did
during five years in the White House. It was hard." Sheehan praises
Albright for not bending to pressures on Boutros-Ghali's behalf. "It
wouldn't have happened without her. She hung in there. It was the
right thing to do."

Even Sheehan is astonished by just how good a Secretary General
Kofi Annan has been. "I don't think anyone foresaw that level of
greatness. We knew he was solid, we knew he was good, we liked him,
we trusted him, we respected him. I don't think anyone would dream
that he would rise to this stature, but we'll take credit anyway for
foreseeing it."

But was it right? Should a dominant nation be able to decide that it doesn't like the Secretary General and methodically force him out? Our UN insider has no problem with that, though faulting the reasons offered by the US government. "The Americans were right to get rid of Boutros but not on the ground that he wasn't reforming the UN. The official reason they gave was that he was resistant to reform, which was nonsense. In fact he did want reform more than anyone else. He may have done it in a way that we, the staff, didn't like, but he decisively slashed posts, slashed high-level functions, really did reform."

The real reason for Boutros-Ghali's ouster, the insider claims, was that he became a political liability in the US presidential election of 1996. "He let the Republicans have a useful piece of ammunition: they said if there's a Republican president, we would not allow our foreign policy to be made by an un-elected Egyptian bureaucrat sitting in New York. Of course he wasn't making policy. Of course the Americans could do what they want with Boutros. But perception was bad enough politically for Clinton because what mattered was what people thought the truth was. Clinton was, I think, increasingly convinced that he had to get rid of this liability. Why did he need to give the Republicans a stick to beat him on the head with?"

CHAPTER 15

UN Advocates, Donors, and Friends

The United Nations once dealt only with Governments. By now we know that peace and prosperity cannot be achieved without partnerships involving Governments, international organizations, the business community and civil society. In today's world, we depend on each other.

—Kofi Annan, Secretary General of the United Nations

Aside from Kofi Annan, now an international luminary in his role as UN Secretary General, some of the heads of UN agencies and commissions have shone brightly in their public careers, like Carol Bellamy of UNICEF and Mary Robinson of the Office of the High Commissioner for Human Rights. But there are also other kinds of stars—some more comfortable before a camera or a theater audience, some at home in the corporate boardroom—who have aligned themselves with the UN.

Ted Turner and Bill Gates, for example, don't just applaud the UN but throw money too. Turner singlehandedly endowed the United Nations Foundation (discussed below), while the Bill & Melinda Gates Foundation has pledged tens of millions of dollars for various programs, either as sole donor or as part of a consortium of donors. Gates

Secretary General Kofi Annan with wife, Nane Annan, and UN Goodwill Ambassador actor Michael Douglas on July 4, 2000, in Philadelphia. UN/DPI photo by Eskinder Debebe.

has earmarked $50 million for UNICEF and partners to prevent deficiency in dietary micronutrients. The Gates Foundation is a major player in the effort to develop an AIDS vaccine. In addition, the foundation established the Global Fund for Children's Vaccines, which pledged $750 million over five years to improve the health of children in developing nations by funding immunization efforts.

Peace Messengers and Goodwill Ambassadors

The UN's most visible supporters are probably the forty-odd actors, athletes, and other celebrities who have become official Goodwill Ambassadors, Peace Ambassadors, and Peace Messengers. On their own time they volunteer to travel the world, representing the UN before every imaginable kind of audience and spreading word of its programs and concerns. Some of these celebrity volunteers serve at-large and represent the UN as a whole, while others sign on with a part of the system like the UN Development Program (UNDP), the UN Population Fund (UNFPA), or the UN Children's Fund (UNICEF). Actor Danny Kaye became the first Goodwill Ambassador in 1953, with UNICEF, and Audrey Hepburn joined shortly afterward. Soon there were many more: actor Peter Ustinov, singers Harry Belafonte and Judy Collins, and actresses Vanessa Redgrave and Linda Gray. Today, Angelina Jolie is working to help refugees. High-profile helpers come from everywhere: from China, singer Leon Lai; from Italy, actors Lino Banfi and Simona Marchini; from Greece, singer Nana Mouskouri; from Portugal, actress Catarina Furtado.

Peace Ambassador Luciano Pavarotti has raised money for the UN's refugee agency, including some $2 million at one event for Angolan refugees. Actor Danny Glover has toured widely in Africa promoting development, and Mia Farrow has campaigned for polio immunization.

The United Nations Foundation

On Sept. 18, 1997, businessman and philanthropist Ted Turner made an unprecedented gesture when he announced a $1 billion gift in support of UN causes. His historic donation was made in the form of Time-Warner stock, given in ten annual installments. In response to Turner's gift, the UN Foundation (UNF) was created for "promoting a more peaceful, prosperous, and just world," which it seeks by publicizing and funding various UN activities. Its four main functions are to (1) provide additional funding for programs and people served by UN agencies; (2) help forge new partnerships between UN agencies, the private sector, and nongovernmental organizations in order to improve support for the UN while also enhancing the effectiveness of service delivery; (3) in cooperation with a sister organization, the Better World Fund, sponsor or conduct efforts aimed at educating the public about the UN's unique role in addressing global issues; and (4) encourage public and private donors to help demonstrate what the UN and the world can do when the public and private sectors cooperate and co-invest.

An example of how these goals play out in the real world can be seen in the Adopt-A-Minefield campaign. In many parts of the world the land is sewn with small land mines, relics of civil wars and other violent outbreaks that remain lethal to humans long after the fighting has ended. The mines are invisible and their location is seldom known with accuracy. The UN agency most involved in clearing mines is the UNDP, which has collaborated with the Better World Fund and the UNA-USA (see below) to sponsor "Adopt-A-Minefield," enabling companies or individuals to pay for mine removal in more than 100 locations. Costs vary considerably, from $27,000 to clear a village of land mines in Croatia to $34,000 for a field in Cambodia.

The UNF also funds "UNWire," which compiles press stories and original reporting about the UN and makes them available online (*www.unwire.org*). In addition, as noted earlier, Turner also personally provided $34 million to cover the shortfall caused by the reduction in the US scale of assessments to the 2001 regular UN budget. The UNF is active and visible, ready to ride the next economic boom into humanitarian good deeds.

United Nations Association of the United States of America

For those of us who haven't yet made our first billion, an excellent way to participate (at least indirectly) is to join the United Nations Association of the United States of America (UNA-USA), a nonpartisan, nonprofit group. About 23,000 Americans belong to UNA-USA, the country's largest grassroots foreign policy organization, which seeks to educate Americans about the issues facing the UN and to encourage support for strong US leadership in the UN. It is a leading center of policy research on the UN and generally promotes participation in global issues. It offers forums and seminars about major international issues, and helps coordinate the Model United Nations (see Appendix D), an innovative simulation in which students act the roles of diplomats. It also reaches out to the business community through its Business Council for the United Nations. The headquarters of UNA-USA is in New York City, with chapters in more than a hundred other cities. They can be reached at their website (*www.unausa.org*) or by phone (212.907.1300).

Probably the best known program of UNA-USA is the Model United Nations, which the UNA-USA website describes (using a fine oxymoron) as "an authentic simulation" of the General Assembly and other bodies. This program catapults students into the world of diplomacy and negotiation, encouraging them to "step into the shoes of ambassadors from U.N. members states to debate current issues on the organization's vast agenda." Playing the role of delegates, students draft resolutions, "negotiate with supporters and adversaries, resolve conflicts, and navigate the U.N.'s rules of procedures," with the goal of focusing "international cooperation" to solve problems that affect almost every country on earth. A twist on the Model UN is the Global Classrooms program, which brings the simulation into the classroom through curriculum units designed for grades seven through twelve. The curriculum materials include a teacher's guide and an accompanying student workbook.

The Business Council for the United Nations (BCUN) reaches out to the private sector through meetings and partnerships. Through the BCUN, business owners and managers learn about the UN and world issues, and gain access to the largest diplomatic community in the world. The council cites its value in promoting investment flow to the developing world and helping to bridge the "digital divide."

The Academic Council on the United Nations System (ACUNS) is another UN-friendly organization, created to encourage education, writing, and research that contribute to the understanding of international issues and promotion of global cooperation. A primary goal is to strengthen the study of international organizations and to foster ties among academics, the UN system, and international organizations. The ACUNS was created in 1987 at Dartmouth College as an international association of scholars, teachers, practitioners, and others who study or are active in the United Nations system and international organizations. Ongoing projects include research and policy workshops, an annual meeting about UN and international issues, a summer workshop for younger scholars and practitioners hosted in cooperation with the American Society for International Law (ASIL), and a dissertation awards program. The organization also co-sponsors an email discussion listserv with the International Organization section of the International Studies Association (ISA). The ACUNS website is: *www.acuns.wlu.ca/.*

CHAPTER 16

Keeping Tabs on How Nations Vote

A country's voting record in the United Nations is only one dimension of its relations with the United States. . . . Nevertheless, a country's behavior at the United Nations is always relevant in its bilateral relationship with the United States, a point the Secretary of State regularly makes in letters of instruction to new U.S. ambassadors.   —US Department of State

We are hardly surprised to learn that because the US is the biggest player at the UN, its words, actions, and nonactions are parsed a hundred different ways by the world's media, governments, and analysts. But the public is not generally aware that the US government does its own parsing of member states' behavior, especially their voting record in the General Assembly and the Security Council. Section 406 of Public Law 101–246 requires that the State Department inform Congress annually about how UN member states have voted in comparison with how the US has voted on the same issues.

Each year, the State Department's UN analysts tote up all the issues, all the votes, and then examine them according to several criteria, such as the geographical distribution of the member states (Europe, Asia, etc.) or their tendency to vote with or contrary to the US voting position.

Table 4 General Assembly Voting Coincidence with the US, 1995–2000, for Issues Resolved not by Consensus but by a Vote

Year	Arms Control	Middle East	Human Rights	Overall Votes
2000	66.1%	11.9%	55.7%	43.0%
1999	57.9	22.7	52.5	41.8
1998	64.0	22.5	62.8	44.2
1997	65.8	26.2	61.9	46.7
1996	62.3	28.3	68.3	49.4
1995	60.9	35.2	81.0	50.6

Source: US Department of State, *18th Annual Report on Voting Practices in the UN,* 2000, p. 2.

The most recent such State Department report covers the UN for calendar year 2000. The 55th General Assembly adopted 275 resolutions, 209 (76 percent) by consensus. The really interesting numbers concern the nonconsensus issues, where a vote was taken, because these reflect how nations may differ from the US position. As Table 4 shows, the overall rate of voting coincidence declined over the six-year period, particularly regarding the Middle East and human rights, two areas where the US has historically taken strong positions that do not always find broad international support.

Information on how individual nations voted is available elsewhere in the State Department report (available at *www.state.gov/plio/conrpt/ vtgprac*). The report finds, among other things, that Israel almost always voted with the US, and the UK was not far behind. But among the sixteen countries that voted with the US less than 25 percent of the time were several obvious suspects like Libya, Cuba, and North Korea, and a few surprises like Egypt and Pakistan.

When we move to the Security Council, there is no suspense about the numbers. The tight club almost always acts through consensus. Of some fifty resolutions adopted in 2000, forty-three (86 percent) were adopted unanimously. John Negroponte sees the numbers as clear proof that "for all the talk about how people worry about the US

The voting board in the General Assembly in 1974. UN photo by T. Chen.

and our being unilateral, the number of resolutions and issues that we succeed in dealing with on a totally consensus basis is really quite striking."

But what do these numbers mean in terms of US foreign policy? As the report observes, although a nation's UN voting record "is only one dimension of its relations with the US," it is nevertheless a significant factor and "always relevant to its bilateral relationship with the US." The report goes on to say, "The SC and the GA are arguably the most important international bodies in the world, dealing as they do with such vital issues as threats to peace and security, disarmament, development, humanitarian relief, human rights, the environment, and narcotics—all of which can and do directly affect major US interests." The State Department gives copies of the report to the foreign ministries and UN missions of UN member states, as a friendly reminder that Uncle Sam is watching.

CHAPTER 17

Making a Career at the UN

We were dealing with actual human beings, and I could put my head to the pillow at night knowing that what I did made a real difference in people's lives—people I could see and feel and meet and touch and actually talk to. That kind of direct connection, that's something that UNHCR affords that's truly extraordinary.

—Shashi Tharoor, UN Undersecretary General for Communications and Public Information

To put a face on the career UN staffer, it's helpful to listen as one of them talks about his early years in the UN as an idealistic young administrator out to learn about the world. Shashi Tharoor was born in India, educated there and in the US, and in 1978 became a staff member of the UN High Commissioner for Refugees (UNHCR), which assists refugees in resettling. He was sent to Singapore (1981–84) to help organize efforts to aid the thousands of Vietnamese fleeing their homeland in the aftermath of the collapse of the Saigon government and the takeover of the country by the Communists in 1975. From 1989 to 1996, Tharoor was part of the peacekeeping office of the

Secretariat as a special assistant to the Under-Secretary General for Peacekeeping Operations. In 2002 he became Undersecretary General for Communications and Public Information. In an interview at his UN office Tharoor recalled his challenging work as a new staff member of the UNHCR:

The High Commissioner for Refugees was a great place to begin my career because it really attracts a lot of idealists, in those days in particular. What really brought me to a conviction of the indispensability of the UN was working for UNHCR in the field. I arrived in Singapore at the peak of the Vietnamese boat-people crisis. There were 4,000 refugees living at the camp, sleeping 25, 30 to a room this size. The situation had become totally unmanageable. When refugees left Vietnam by boat, they were picked up by boats sailing into Singapore. The Singapore government was very unhappy about having refugees come in, and they manifested this by making difficult the disembarkation of some of these refugees and having nothing to do with the camps themselves. Other countries who were receiving Vietnamese refugees ran their own camps, usually with their military, whereas in Singapore the UN was asked to run their camps.

UNHCR in those days believed it was not an operational agency, so we weren't supposed to be running camps. It was an extraordinary challenge for someone who was in their twenties as I was. I essentially invented operational partners by going to churches and church groups and saying, "Put your label on us and say you're the operational partner, and I will raise money to get the staff and we will run the camp." I got volunteers from the city, including wives of diplomats, to come in and teach refugees and run camps. I took donations from the community for the benefit of the refugees. I got refugees to run their own democracy, elect their own camp leader.

On the diplomatic side, there was dealing with a tough government, trying to use the power of my office to get them to cooperate. Church groups can go and help refugees, volunteers can go and help refugees, but only the UN can go to a government. I would tell officials, "You

Vietnamese refugees, often called "boat people," are rescued in the South China Sea in 1975. UNHCR/1505 photo by P. Deloche.

have an obligation to honor your international commitment to this organization." Even if they're not signatories to the UN convention, as a member of the General Assembly they're bound by the statute of the organization, which is a General Assembly resolution. We expect them to honor their role as a government and a member of the UN.

We had to invent whole new procedures. For example when ships came in, [the authorities] insisted that every ship that had refugees had to provide a guarantee that the refugees would be resettled. Then they realized that some of the guarantees were worthless because some of the ships were from Bangladesh and India and flag-of-convenience ships flying the Liberian flag or the Panamanian flag. What use was a letter of guarantee from Liberia that they will resettle their refugees?

The Singaporeans then wanted a letter from a country of resettlement. We had to invent a scheme, where we had looked into the ownership of a ship, and got a country of registration to actually provide the guarantees, and then there were the weekly meetings in my office with the immigration chiefs of embassies. It's a sobering thought that there are kids growing up French, or Canadian, or American today because of my skill or lack thereof in persuading an immigration officer to bend the rules.

Every month more were arriving, I would imagine somewhere between 12,000 and 20,000 refugees passed through my hands in Singapore. In one case, for example, a family left for Singapore on a tiny boat with a cannibalized tractor engine. It wasn't a proper motor and sure enough it conked out and they were drifting on the high seas. They ran out of food, out of water, and they were subsisting on rainwater and hope. What do the parents do? They slit their fingers to get their babies to suck their own blood in order to survive. They were finally rescued by an American ship and they were so weak they couldn't stand up, they had to be lifted out of the boat. We rushed them into intensive care in the hospital as soon as we could disembark them. Now, to see that same family three or four months later, healthy, well fed, well rested, well dressed, heading off to new lives in the US, there is simply no job that could compare with that sort of thing—pure human satisfaction.

When Poland declared martial law in December of 1981, do you remember the Solidarity movement [labor union] and all of that? A Polish ship docked in Singapore on a Saturday and four or five Polish seamen jumped ship and looked up the UN in the phone book and came to my office and wanted asylum. I had no authority to grant asylum. I woke up the director of international protections of the UNHCR and said, "What do I do?" The guy said, "Follow the convention, interview these people, and determine if in your view they should have refugee status. If you do, they are refugees."

It was quite a drama. I interviewed them. I felt that they had a credible case. They said they were supporters of Solidarity and if they went back they would be locked up, so they jumped ship. I said, "I recognize you as refugees," and basically said to the Singaporeans, "You've got to let these people stay." The Singaporeans were furious, but I contacted some embassies and said, "Could you try and take these people?" We worked out a scheme. The Singaporeans retaliated by banning shore leave for all Polish seamen. They kept saying, "You are only here to look after the Vietnamese." And I said, "No, I'm with the UN High Commissioner for Refugees. Vietnamese happen to be my caseload, but anybody else who comes in, I'm legally mandated under the statute of the office to help them."

A couple of months after this first episode, I got a frantic call from the Singaporeans and the Americans, one after the other. A Polish sailor had jumped ship, swum to an American destroyer in the port. Singapore naval police and immigration police said he had to be handed over because he was illegal. The American captain said that the sailor was fleeing communism and he would not surrender him. There was a diplomatic standoff. Neither side wanted this to hit the press, but the Singaporeans wouldn't let the American ship sail with the Polish seaman on board, and the Polish seaman couldn't go back to his ship. The Americans allowed the Singaporeans to take him off the ship under the condition that he be brought to me. He was brought to the US consul's office in the embassy, where it was determined he had refugee status, at which point we took charge and put him in a little hotel in Singapore (where it's not an inexpensive proposition for the UN, I can tell you).

Then I started putting heat on the Americans, saying, "Take him because we solved the problem for you and you have to resettle him." It dragged on for a couple of months before the US agreed to take him. A new consul arrived and was very helpful and said that he would take charge.

I got a lovely postcard from San Diego from this Polish seaman, saying, "I never will forget you, Mr. Shashi." One of the precious souvenirs of my career!

Singapore was such an extraordinary period, and among other things it convinced me about the indispensability of the UN cause. Most things I've done under the UN, only the UN could have done. The UN has a hell of a lot of advantages in dealing with authorities. There are so many stories in which the governmental influence that the UN can bring to bear changes the lives and fortunes of people who are in danger or distress.

CHAPTER 18

ECOSOC

The worst two years of my life were spent as Canada's representative on ECOSOC. A complete waste of time.

—David Malone, former Canadian diplomat and
Director of the International Peace Academy

A quick look at the UN organizational chart reveals that one of the Principal Organs—in fact, the only one we haven't discussed yet—is something called Economic and Social Council (ECOSOC). ECOSOC is a key coordinator and mediator among the constituent bodies of the UN system. But it has struggled to find a clear identity among its many functions and as a result has been accused of being unfocused. David Malone's comment above is not unique; others have also remarked on ECOSOC's talent for fostering endless debate that leads to no apparent action. Admittedly, ECOSOC was created to be mainly a deliberative rather than operational body, to help other parts of the UN system examine and shape their programs. In addition to being a forum for discussing international social, economic, and humanitarian issues, it coordinates the work of nearly all UN agencies and bodies concerned with those issues. As part of its coordinating role,

From the UN Charter, Chapter X:
The Economic and Social Council

ARTICLE 62

1. The Economic and Social Council may make or initiate studies and reports with respect to international economic, social, cultural, educational, health, and related matters and may make recommendations with respect to any such matters to the General Assembly, to the Members of the United Nations, and to the specialized agencies concerned.
2. It may make recommendations for the purpose of promoting respect for, and observance of, human rights and fundamental freedoms for all.
3. It may prepare draft conventions for submission to the General Assembly, with respect to matters falling within its competence.
4. It may call, in accordance with the rules prescribed by the United Nations, international conferences on matters falling within its competence.

ARTICLE 63

1. The Economic and Social Council may enter into agreements with any of the agencies referred to in Article 57, defining the terms on which the agency concerned shall be brought into relationship with the United Nations. Such agreements shall be subject to approval by the General Assembly.
2. It may coordinate the activities of the specialized agencies through consultation with and recommendations to such agencies and through recommendations to the General Assembly and to the Members of the United Nations.

ARTICLE 71

The Economic and Social Council may make suitable arrangements for consultation with non-governmental organizations which are concerned with matters within its competence. Such arrangements may be made with international organizations and, where appropriate, with national organizations after consultation with the Member of the United Nations concerned.

ECOSOC commissions studies, writes reports, and makes policy recommendations to the General Assembly and other parts of the UN.
Membership in ECOSOC—which holds a major session every July—
is coveted, owing to the body's central role in the UN universe. Its
fifty-four members, elected by the General Assembly, serve three-year
terms.

Flirting with Irrelevance?

Perhaps because its mission is so extensive, and it does a lot of coordinating among groups and organizations, ECOSOC lacks a clear public
profile and has suffered from a lack of conceptual and administrative
focus. It is almost everything but not exactly anything. Many diplomats, like David Malone, have found the organization's fuzziness and
endless discussions hard to endure. This has produced a plethora
of recommendations for reworking the body. Malone's advice is for
ECOSOC to make itself more relevant to the UN by working closely
with the Security Council on a vital issue, such as peace-building.
Peace-building involves addressing the causes of violence rather than
the deadly effects. It has particular relevance to today's world, where
so much violence occurs within nations rather than between them.
Peace-building involves strengthening basic civil institutions and the
rule of law, promoting respect for human rights, and rebuilding administrative and economic infrastructure. Many of the activities of
peace-building are actually done by UN agencies, nongovernmental
organizations and other organizations, frequently under the umbrella
of a Security Council peacekeeping mission. Malone thinks the Security Council would be open to having ECOSOC take the leading role
in peace-building but that ECOSOC "has yet to pick up the challenge."

Nongovernmental Organizations

One of ESOSOC's most important and delicate functions is to act as
intermediary between the General Assembly and nongovernmental
organizations (NGOs), which are independent, nonprofit, voluntary

The ECOSOC chamber. UN/DPI photo by Andrea Brizzi.

associations that focus on one or more areas of interest to the UN, such as human rights or environmental protection. In the United States, we usually refer to them as "nonprofit organizations" because we make a sharp distinction between private enterprise (which is profit-making) and civil society (which is not), but in most of the world, where the crucial distinction is between governmental and nongovernmental, NGO makes more sense as a category. (Outside the US, business is often included in civil society, again because the crucial distinction is between governmental versus nongovernmental.)

The UN has taken a growing interest in NGOs because they represent the interests of civil society, which is gaining visibility as a foundation of democracy. Kofi Annan recently acknowledged the importance of creating partnerships between the UN and civil society to achieve "a new synthesis between private initiative and the public good, which encourages entrepreneurship and market approaches together with social and environmental responsibility."

ECOSOC negotiates the agreements that define relations between the UN and the nearly 2,200 NGOs that have "consultative status," which gives them the right to participate in certain types of UN meetings, studies, and projects, and to submit reports to ECOSOC. When the UN was founded there were only a few NGOs, but in recent decades the number has risen dramatically, and they have become crucial in helping implement many important programs such as those related to human rights, literacy, health care, and economic development. More than 20,000 transnational NGOs existed in 1996, and the average nation now has almost 500 of them, compared with fewer than 20 per nation back in 1960.

A Public-Private Partnership

"NGOs play a more and more important role not only in the policy debates but equally important, maybe even more important, are critical in implementing many of these policies. A lot of the aid and emergency humanitarian assistance, like food distribution by the World Food Program, is done through the NGOs. There really is a public-private partnership, or a public-NGO partnership, that is very important. NGOs are effective, and part of the reason is they are private and they are accountable, they watch their pennies. People have a choice as to whom to give their money."
—John Negroponte, US Ambassador to the UN

Human rights NGOs such as Amnesty International and Human Rights Watch attend the meetings of the UN's Human Rights Commission, participate in the discussions, and submit reports on matters that concern them. NGOs have their own liaison body, the Conference on Non-Governmental Organizations in Consultative Status (CONGO), to represent their interests before ECOSOC and hold meetings about issues of common interest. Those NGOs holding consultative status remain independent bodies and do not become actual parts of the UN. To the contrary, their influence often depends on their reputation for independence from outside authority.

CHAPTER 19

Agencies, Programs, and Commissions

Article 55
With a view to the creation of conditions of stability and well-being which are necessary for peaceful and friendly relations among nations based on respect for the principle of equal rights and self-determination of peoples, the United Nations shall promote:
a. higher standards of living, full employment, and conditions of economic and social progress and development;
b. solutions of international economic, social, health, and related problems; and international cultural and educational cooperation; and
c. universal respect for, and observance of, human rights and fundamental freedoms for all without distinction as to race, sex, language, or religion.
—UN Charter

The Secretariat, Security Council, General Assembly, and other Principal Organs are the UN bodies that most command the public's attention. Yet, they have only general oversight of the UN's huge array of global efforts to advance human rights, help refugees or earthquake victims, combat infectious diseases, or coordinate international trade, finance, development, and communications. The direct control of these vital activities is usually in the hands of entities known as agencies, programs, and commissions, which make up the UN's less publicly exposed side. And, although these groups remain mostly in the background, they play key roles in the UN system. Some of the agencies, for example, actually pre-date the UN, and many act quite independently.

These supporting entities consist of nearly sixty organizations, divided into six categories. Moving from left to right on the UN organizational chart (see Chapter 1), we see first the Programs and Funds. Each of these was created to address a particular issue the General Assembly has deemed important. That is true also for the next category, Other UN Entities, such as the Office of the High Commissioner for Human Rights, and for the Research and Training Institutes, such as the International Research and Training Institute for the Advancement of Women (INSTRAW). Moving to the upper right we have the Commissions, of two types, Functional and Regional. The remaining two boxes contain the Related Organizations and the Specialized Agencies, which are autonomous organizations that have formal working relations with the UN. You can see from their names that the related organizations and specialized agencies cover virtually all areas of economic and social endeavor.

Coordination of these organizations is one of the greatest challenges facing the UN, for they have offices all over the map, with thousands of staff of all nationalities, and they address every imaginable issue. As a further complication, the categories of organizations each relate to the UN in a different way. The Administrative Committee on Coordination is charged with choreographing this ungainly ensemble.

To an outsider, these supporting organizations all look pretty much the same. Only the insider can perceive and fully appreciate their differences in terms of administrative position and prerogatives. The public, however, is more interested in the basics: what they do and how they do it. To find out what and how, a functional approach is best, because the organizations share many interests and methods of operation.

In a nutshell, the UN helps keep peace, promotes human rights, protects the environment, fights poverty, discourages nuclear proliferation, strengthens international law, provides humanitarian aid, promotes democracy, advances women's rights and human rights, provides safe drinking water, eradicates disease, promotes education, reduces child mortality, and improves global communications.

There are many ways of defining the major issues addressed by the agencies, programs, and commissions. The UN has its own ideas about how to describe the issues that shape their agendas. For example, at the Millennium Summit, Kofi Annan divided the UN's work into four broad areas: freedom from want, freedom from fear, a sustainable future, and renewal of the UN.

Rather than use the UN's categories, I prefer to identify a set of issues relevant to the average reader: first are human rights, followed by the related areas of economic and social development, then the natural environment. Next comes disaster relief, then the control of dangerous agents like toxins and nuclear materials, and finally the UN's role in globalization—first, in shaping world trade; second, in dealing with the expansion of international crime.

I don't claim these categories are definitive, but they do enable us to look at the supporting organizations in a systematic and functional manner. Keep in mind that these entities could easily fill a whole book by themselves. The Further Reading list at the back of this book provides a list of source material for those curious to learn more.

CHAPTER 20

Rule of Law and Human Rights

Strikingly, the centrality of human rights to peoples' expectation about the future role of the United Nations was stressed both at the [Millennium Summit regional] hearings and in the [public opinion] survey. The current level of performance, especially of government, was judged to be unsatisfactory. —Kofi Annan, Secretary General of the UN

Rights come first everywhere you look at the UN. The purpose of the organization, according to Article 1 of the Charter, is to promote and encourage "respect for human rights and for fundamental freedoms for all without distinction as to race, sex, language, or religion." The Universal Declaration of Human Rights, as we saw earlier, is literally all about rights (see Appendix B). Nearly all states that join the UN have agreed to accept its principles through the signing and ratifying of two international covenants, one addressing civil and political rights and the other economic, social, and cultural rights. The International Covenant on Civil and Political Rights and the International Covenant on Economic, Social, and Cultural Rights, which entered force in 1976, are legally binding documents. When combined with the Universal Declaration, they constitute the International Bill of Human Rights.

In addition, most member states have signed and ratified some eighty treaties that cover particular aspects of human rights. To give an idea of what they cover, here are only a few, with their initiation dates:

1948 Convention on the Prevention and Punishment of the Crime of Genocide

1961 Convention Relating to the Status of Refugees

1965 International Convention on the Elimination of All Forms of Racial Discrimination

1984 Convention Against Torture and Other Cruel, Inhuman or Degrading Treatment or Punishment

1990 International Convention on the Protection of the Rights of All Migrant Workers and Members of Their Families

The UN is justifiably proud of having enabled the creation of such wide-ranging safeguards of human rights. It has, additionally, been able to use its influence and authority to improve human rights in some nations, such as South Africa. There the UN led an anti-Apartheid campaign, including an arms embargo, that helped end official racial segregation. It then sent an observer mission in 1994 that monitored free elections and facilitated the transition away from official segregation.

A Commission and a High Commissioner

All offices and staff of the UN and its peacekeeping operations are responsible for adhering to international human rights law and reporting possible breaches of it to the proper authorities, but several have a special responsibility for rights. We have already seen how creation of the International Criminal Court (ICC), for example, will make permanent the capacity for investigating and prosecuting large-scale crimes against humanity.

The Commission on Human Rights, created in 1946, is the main body for making policy and providing a forum for discussion. It meets for six weeks each year in Geneva, Switzerland, and holds public meetings on violations of human rights. In 1993, the General Assembly

From the UN Charter, Chapter III: Organs

ARTICLE 8

The United Nations shall place no restrictions on the eligibility of men and women to participate in any capacity and under conditions of equality in its principal and subsidiary organs.

established the post of UN High Commissioner for Human Rights (HCHR), to provide a secretariat for the commission and to oversee the UN's human rights activities, help develop rights standards, and promote international cooperation to expand and protect rights. The current High Commissioner is Sergio Vieira de Mello.

The reports of the Human Rights Commission probe the status of rights in specific countries and hold them accountable for how they treat their citizens. The commission has the option of censuring nations with poor human rights records, but that happens on a selective basis that is heavily influenced by politics on the commission. For example, many experts on human rights rate China's record in this area as very poor, and the US representatives on the commission have long urged an investigation of China's human rights record, yet the commission has not acted. In 2001, for example, the commission adopted resolutions condemning rights violations in Afghanistan, Burma, Burundi, Chechnya, Congo, Cuba, Iran, Rwanda, and Sierra Leone—but not China.

When necessary, the Human Rights Commission appoints experts, called special rapporteurs, to examine rights abuses or conditions in specific countries. In some cases, when an international rights convention enters force, the UN may create a watchdog committee charged with ensuring that the treaty provisions are honored by member states. For example, when the Convention on the Rights of the Child entered force in 1989, it was accompanied by the creation of the Committee on the Rights of the Child, which meets regularly and has become an

Rights Hotline

The UN Office of Commission on Human Rights, in Geneva, Switzerland, maintains a 24-hour fax hotline to report violations of human
rights. The number is 41 22 917 0092.

international voice for children. Other committees created to monitor
specific conventions are the

Committee on the Elimination of Racial Discrimination
Committee on Economic, Social, and Cultural Rights
Committee Against Torture
Committee on the Elimination of Discrimination Against Women

   Periodically the UN identifies groups that merit attention because
their rights have been abridged. For example, the Secretary General
has appointed Olara Otunnu as a Special Representative for Children
in Armed Conflict—in other words, an advocate for child soldiers.
Again, in 1993, the UN launched the International Year of the World's
Indigenous People as a way of calling attention to the rights (and other
needs) of groups like India's Tribals and Peru's Indians, who have
suffered various forms of social, economic, and legal discrimination.
Often these "Year of . . ." events lead to follow-up activities that may
produce international treaties, as happened with children in 1989, as
noted above. The UN regards rights as so important that it has given
them not their own year but their own decade, the UN Decade for
Human Rights Education (1995–2004).

Mainstreaming Human Rights

Earlier we touched on Secretary General Kofi Annan's "rights-based"
approach to development, which highlights the importance of human
rights as a positive and necessary component to social and economic
progress. If the UN can "mainstream" human rights issues as part of

the broader development agenda, it may achieve a breakthrough, because then rights would be seen not simply as a noble addition to society but as integral to it.

The rise of an international women's rights agenda offers a possible mainstreaming model. Experts in development are now arguing that society benefits greatly when women can take control of their work, property, and bodies. The UN has been advancing this line of thought through a variety of mechanisms, and although progress has been slow and uneven among nations, much has changed during the past few decades. The UN's constant publicizing of women's issues has contributed to a growing consensus among experts that rights are good for everyone.

For women, as with anyone else, the exercise of rights begins with an understanding of what "rights" are. The Preamble to the Universal Declaration specifies gender equality as a basic right. Even before the Declaration was finished, the UN had established the Commission on the Status of Women, which meets regularly and makes recommendations and suggests international legislation about women's rights. The UN's impact also comes through its public awareness campaigns and its major conferences. Soon after the surfacing of the women's movement during the late 1960s and early '70s, the UN declared 1975 to be International Women's Year and 1976–1985 the UN Decade for Women. The momentum generated by these efforts led to adoption in 1979 of the Convention on the Elimination of All Forms of Discrimination Against Women (CEDAW). This has been described as both "an international bill of rights for women" and "a blueprint for action by countries to guarantee those rights."

Complementing these public relations measures, the UN convened the first global conference ever held on women (in Mexico City), followed by world conferences in Copenhagen (1980), Nairobi (1985), and Beijing (1995). UN Conferences often attract high-profile delegations from most of the world's nations. A major purpose of the conference is to agree on a set of shared principles or an agenda for action (often referred to as a "platform for action") for the years until the next major conference. At Beijing, for example, the US delegation was led by then First Lady Hillary Rodham Clinton, who gave one of the major addresses. The conference produced the Beijing Declaration and Platform for Action.

Five years later, the General Assembly conducted Beijing +5, a review of the platform. In preparation for the review, the Commission on the Status of Women met in New York City in February and March 2000. With due ceremony, the General Assembly special session met from June 5 through 9, 2000, with Secretary of State Madeleine Albright chairing the US delegation and Secretary of Health and Human Services Donna Shalala and US Permanent Rep Richard Holbrooke co-chairing. Among outcomes of the session was a review of gains and hindrances in advancing the status of women worldwide.

Leading UN Actors

Most organizations within the UN system deal with human rights in one way or another, but several have special competence in this area. Note that some of those listed below are not focused fully on human rights but are included here because their goals are closely connected with rights issues.

- The Commission on Human Rights was established in 1946 and is based in Geneva, Switzerland.
  The commission makes policy, commissions studies, and monitors human rights worldwide. URL: *www.unhcr.ch*
- The Office of the High Commissioner for Human Rights (OHCHR), created in 1993, is based in Geneva, Switzerland. URL: *www.unhcr.ch*
  The OHCHR has principal responsibility for UN human rights activities. The first High Commissioner was Jose Ayala-Lasso of Ecuador, who was succeeded in 1997 by Mary Robinson, former President of Ireland. The OHCHR has staff in about 30 countries, who provide technical services, monitor rights, and investigate alleged rights abuses (more than 100,000 annually).

- The Commission on the Status of Women, established in 1946, is based in New York. URL: *www.un.org/womenwatch/daw/csw/*
  The commission promotes implementation of equal rights for women and men.
- The International Research and Training Institute for the Advancement of Women (INSTRAW), established in 1976, is headquartered in Santo Domingo, Dominican Republic. URL: *www.un-instraw.org*
  INSTRAW is an autonomous body of the UN governed by an ECOSOC-appointed 11-member board of trustees. INSTRAW supports women's full participation in the economic, social, and political spheres through training, research, and information.
- UN Development Fund for Women (UNIFEM), created in 1976, is based in New York City and works closely with the UN Development Program (UNDP). URL: *www.unifem.undp.org*
  UNIFEM funds innovative development activities to benefit women, especially in rural areas of the developing world.

CHAPTER 21

Social and Economic Development

We know the answers to development problems, it's often just a matter of applying them and implementing them. We've had huge successes. Life expectancy has gone up, fewer kids are dying, more kids are in school. But poverty is still a huge problem out there. Money matters, but so do ideas and partnerships and consensus-building politics and all the things the UN's good at. —Mark Malloch Brown, Administrator of the UNDP

The word "development" has undergone an amazing rise in popularity in recent years, owing largely to its association with an even more popular word, "globalization." Globalization has raised our awareness that the level of the wealth among nations differs greatly, for reasons that are often hard to identify. This variation has renewed an old debate about why some nations develop rapidly while others seem hardly to change at all. The UN is a big player in development through its programs and agencies, including the World Bank. These bodies have mandates to pay special attention to the poorest nations.

The international debate about the pace of development has often pitted the poor nations against the rich, with the poor ones claiming

A homeless couple huddles by railroad track in Jakarta, Indonesia, in 1986.
UN photo 155256 by John Isaac.

they are the victims of an oppressive global system that prevents them
from escaping debt and poverty. Experts are increasingly agreeing
with this analysis, at least in one sense. There is growing consensus
that the old approach to economic development no longer works well.
It is not enough just to raise the level of economic growth and assume
that all boats will be lifted by the rising tide. "Old-school prescriptions
of supplementing rapid growth with social spending and safety nets
have proved inadequate," one recent UN report noted. In addition,
many experts are advising that governments need to be more accountable to their citizens, who should have a significant role in running
anti-poverty programs.

Mark Malloch Brown is head of the UN Development Program
(UNDP), one of the leading bodies in the development effort. He
emphasizes the need to strengthen the internal capacity of nations
rather than trying to insert infrastructure or industry into a nation

without taking into account its social and economic context. Malloch Brown defines development as, "How the hell do you make sense of countries where they are not training people, where there are not strong institutions? Managing one's response to that with some prudent capacity-building, institution-building, and training of people before throwing money . . . is incredibly important." He cautions that development "is not a linear thing where you see human suffering and you throw money at it and suffering is solved." Rather, both developing nations and those who assist them, like the UNDP, should invest in people through education, health, and making space for a strong private sector, with suitable rewards along the way in the shape of aid from the World Bank and other donors. This process, he believes, can help move a nation from dependency on World Bank loans to establishment of private investment flows. "It's a ladder you go up, from the early UNDP help."

Kofi Annan has pushed the UN to examine and embrace the new thinking. He wants an emphasis on sustainable development rather than the single-minded emphasis on a few aspects such as heavy industry or hydroelectric projects. He wants real poverty reduction and greater input from ordinary people. The UN responded with the Millennium Summit, discussed in Chapter 7, which met in 2000 to debate Annan's proposals as set forth in a special report written by his office. The report suggests initiatives to advance four fundamental goals: freedom from want, freedom from fear, a sustainable future, and renewal of the UN.

Malloch Brown finds an interesting parallel between the goals of the Millennium Summit and the evolution of European and American thinking about social reform and the so-called social safety net. "We are in the early stages of an interesting transformation of what politicians consider their responsibility. Many of the people who were around to form the UN . . . were domestically part of FDR's reforms and Britain's welfare state reforms. But they were too early for the export of their social policies abroad—for a global safety net—and now suddenly the world's ready for their vision of fifty years ago."

Some insiders are less sure that a major change has occurred. They have seen so much "new thinking" fizzle during the past few decades that they remain skeptical or downright hostile to the UN's development effort. This critique argues that many UN bodies, such as the UNDP, are liable to overestimate the ability to influence the pace and scope of development. That is always a danger with large organizations that have a strong top-down bureaucratic perspective, no matter how well-intentioned the executives and staff may be. In addition, competition among organizations for support from donors can lead to inflated claims of effectiveness, according to the critique. Malloch Brown does see cause for optimism because of a waning of the turf battles that have often kept UN bodies from collaborating and maximizing their impact. "The UN has come to a fundamental transition," he says, "from a rather intellectually sterile, politically fierce inside competition to the much more constructive mode where we've made our institutional peace." Now the UNDP accepts the World Bank's long-held emphasis on the need for macroeconomic stability, and the bank accepts the UNDP's focus on social spending and social policy.

But Malloch Brown wants to go further. "You need much more innovative social policy. You don't need just macro economic stability and a social safety net, you need targeted social spending programs which reach vulnerable groups." The key, he argues (echoing Kofi Annan), is to add strategies that "are not economic and social in character, but human rights in character to bring marginal core groups around the world into the mainstream political economy." This is another way of stating the rights-based approach to development, which places the emphasis on individual initiative rather than bureaucratic control. "We've done social spending in a big macro sense and still people are poor. But the center of the political debate, the intellectual debate about development policy, is going to shift back towards the UN with its more holistic view of poverty strategies, which embraces the cultural, the social, and the political, not just the economic."

Leading UN Actors

Among the many UN organizations that participate in the global development effort, several are prominent:

- The UN Development Program (UNDP) is based in New York City and was founded in 1945. URL: *www.undp.org*

  The UNDP concentrates on four aspects of development: poverty, the environment, jobs, and women. Among its many projects, it promotes small businesses in Bulgaria, helps devise development plans in Nepal that include local participation, and helps institutions in Botswana improve their ability to deal with the HIV/AIDS epidemic.

  A recent US government report observed that the UNDP gives the US an "important channel of communication, particularly in countries where the US has no permanent presence." Not surprisingly, the US has been the organization's biggest donor; its allocation for 2002 was $87.1 million. The US has praised Mark Malloch Brown, UNDP Administrator, for making important administrative reforms.

- The Food and Agriculture Organization (FAO) has been operating as a specialized UN agency since 1945, first from Washington, DC, and since 1951 from its headquarters in Rome, Italy. URL: *www.fao.org*

  Most of the FAO's work relates to agriculture in a direct way, such as providing technical assistance about farming or nutrition, but it also tries to address factors like AIDS that significantly affect farming communities. Because most hunger today is the result of political or economic factors rather than poor crops, the FAO has begun concentrating on the effective delivery of food to those who need it. In 2000, for example, it collaborated with the World Bank to provide cattle and farm machinery to jump-start farming in Kosovo. The FAO's statistics on agriculture, forestry, food supplies, nutrition, and fisheries are authoritative and highly regarded. Many countries, including the US, have applauded the FAO's efforts to protect commercial fisheries from overexploitation by developing an international plan of action. In 1996 it hosted the World Food Summit, where 185 nations issued the Rome Declaration on World Food Security and pledged to cut the number of hungry people in half by 2015.

The largest autonomous UN agency, with some 4,300 staff, the FAO has an annual budget of approximately $325 million, of which the US paid about one quarter for 2000.

- The International Fund for Agricultural Development (IFAD), founded in 1977, is a specialized agency of the UN based in Rome, Italy. URL: *www.ifad.org*

IFAD is mandated to combat hunger and rural poverty in developing countries by providing long-term, low-cost loans for projects that improve the nutrition and food supply of small farmers, nomadic herders, landless rural people, poor women, and others. IFAD also encourages other agencies and governments to contribute their own funds to these projects. The agency's largest contributor is the US, which has provided about $575 million since 1977.

- The International Labor Organization (ILO), created in 1919, is based in Geneva, Switzerland. URL: *www.ilo.org*

The ILO formulates international labor standards through conventions and recommendations that establish minimum standards of labor rights, such as the right to organize, collective bargaining, and equality of opportunity and treatment. It also offers technical assistance in vocational training and rehabilitation, employment policy, labor relations, working conditions, and occupational safety and health. One of the ILO's most important functions is to investigate and report on whether member states are adhering to the labor conventions and treaties they have signed. The US, which has a permanent seat on the ILO's governing body, considers the organization vital for addressing exploitative child labor. The ILO's Program for the Elimination of Child Labor was allotted $45 million from the US Congress for 2001, with another $37 million targeted at improving educational access to working children. A recent US government report claims that the programs have "removed tens of thousands of children" in Central America, Bangladesh, Pakistan, and elsewhere "from exploitative work, placed them in schools, and provided their families with alternative income-producing opportunities."

- The UN Industrial Development Organization (UNIDO), which became a specialized agency in 1985, is based in Vienna, Austria. URL: *www.unido.org*

  UNIDO helps developing nations establish economies that are globally competitive while respecting the natural environment. It mediates communication between business and government and works to encourage entrepreneurship and bring all segments of the population, including women, into the labor force. Its staff of 650 includes engineers, economists, and technology and environment specialists. Its budget for 2000–2001 was $133 million.
- The UN Office for Project Services (UNOPS) is headquartered in New York City and was founded in 1973. URL: *www.unops.org*

  UNOPS provides technical services and management for developing nations that seek to boost their economic base. Its staff of approximately 1,100 is providing a way for all the world's nations to tap into the vast industrial, commercial, and business experience and expertise of the developed nations.
- UN Volunteers (UNV), established in 1970 as a subsidiary organ of the UN, is based in Bonn, Germany. URL: *www.unv.org*

  During the past 30 years, more than 20,000 professionals have volunteered through the UNV to work on community-based development projects, humanitarian aid, and the promotion of human rights. In any given year, the organization deploys about 4,000 specialists and field workers.
- The UN Center for Human Settlements (Habitat), created in 1978, is headquartered in Nairobi, Kenya. URL: *www.unchs.org*

  As the world becomes more urbanized, with nearly half of all people living in cities and towns, there is a growing need to find solutions to slums, infectious diseases, and other ills that accompany overcrowding. Habitat describes itself as promoting "sustainable human settlement development through advocacy, policy formulation, capacity-building, knowledge creation, and the strengthening of partnerships between government and civil society." Its technical programs and projects focus on a wide range of urban issues, including poverty reduction, post-disaster reconstruction, and water management. It has a staff of some 240 and an annual budget of about $160 million. At Habitat II, the Second UN Conference on Human Settlements (Istanbul, 1996), delegates approved the Habitat Agenda, in which governments committed themselves to the goals of adequate shelter for all and sustainable urban development.

- The World Bank was established in 1945 with the goal of reducing global poverty by improving the economies of poor nations. URL: *www.worldbank.org*

This bank makes loans to countries, not grants. The loans, amounting to $17 billion in 2001, go only to governments, but in recent years the bank has tried to ensure that local organizations and communities are included in projects in order to increase the chances for success.

The World Bank consists of five parts, all based in Washington, D.C.:

1. The International Bank for Reconstruction and Development began operations in 1946. It offers loans and financial assistance to member states, each of which subscribes an amount of capital based on its economic strength (a total of about $11 billion since 1946). Voting power in the governing body is linked to the subscriptions. Most of its funds come from bonds sold in international capital markets.

2. The International Development Association offers affordable financing, known as credits, to countries with annual per capita incomes of less than $895. Most of the funds come from the governments of richer nations. IDA lends approximately $6 billion annually.

3. The International Finance Corporation is the developing world's largest multilateral source of loan and equity financing for private-sector projects. The corporation encourages the growth of productive business and efficient capital markets, and invests only when it sees an opportunity to complement the role of private investors.

4. The Multilateral Investment Guarantee Agency provides

The UN Secretariat building is lit with the red AIDS ribbon on June 23, 2001, to signify the commitment to the battle against HIV/AIDS. UN/DPI photo by Eskinder Debebe.

guarantees (that is, insurance) to foreign investors in developing countries. The guarantees protect against losses from political and other factors such as expropriation and war.

5. The International Center for Settlement of Investment Disputes provides arbitration or conciliation services in disputes between governments and private foreign investors.

• The World Health Organization (WHO), founded in 1948, is based in Geneva, Switzerland. URL: *www.who.int*

One of the largest specialized agencies, with a staff of about 3,800 and an annual budget of approximately $240 million, WHO is charged with improving health and with the eradication or control of diseases. Probably the organization's best known success is the eradication of smallpox in 1980. Almost eradicated are leprosy and river blindness. WHO has been addressing other destructive infectious diseases such as tuberculosis, malaria, HIV/AIDS, and polio. With six other UN agencies, WHO belongs to the Joint United Nations Program on HIV/AIDS (UNAIDS), described as "the leading advocate for a worldwide response aimed at preventing transmission, providing care and support, reducing the vulnerability of individuals and communities, and alleviating the impact of the epidemic." WHO's global campaign to eradicate polio began in 1988 and has established partnerships with governments and NGOs. It has reduced the number of cases worldwide to only a few thousand (from 350,000 in 1988) and is expected to achieve eradication by 2005 if adequate funding can be found. Immunizing entire populations against especially deadly diseases is an important part of the WHO program. From 1980 through 1995 it collaborated with UNICEF in a campaign to immunize against polio, tetanus, measles, whooping cough, diphtheria, and tuberculosis. In 1999 it received startup funding from the Bill & Melinda Gates Foundation to establish the Global Alliance for Vaccines and Immunization, which is providing immunization against two major killers, hepatitis B and haemophilus influenza type B.

CHAPTER 22

Protecting the Biosphere and Its Inhabitants

We are failing to provide the freedom of future generations to sustain their lives on this planet.   —Kofi Annan, Secretary General of the UN

Concern for the natural environment has moved up on everyone's agenda over the past three decades, as rapid population increases and economic development have strained the world's forests, farmlands, atmosphere, rivers, and oceans. The UN has taken the lead through its efforts to safeguard our natural heritage. This is an area where the UN's global reach and ability to act as an honest broker has produced impressive results.

The Biosphere

The Earth Summit and the Kyoto Protocol are two UN-sponsored events that have helped transform how we think about our responsibility to the natural environment. The 1992 Conference on Environment and Development, commonly known as the Earth Summit, met in Rio de Janeiro and adopted Agenda 21, a plan for global sustainable development that is being monitored by a UN body, the Commission

on Sustainable Development. Five years after the summit, the General
Assembly held a special session, Earth Summit +5, to assess progress
(which was very uneven) and suggest further action.

The Kyoto Protocol addresses global warming caused by human
action. By the 1990s, a scientific consensus was emerging that carbon
dioxide and other "greenhouse gases" emitted largely by industrialized nations were causing the world's climate to warm, with potentially serious long-term consequences for vital human activities such
as agriculture. One-fifth of the world's inhabitants were producing
about 60 percent of annual carbon dioxide emissions, the largest
offender being the United States. Delegates at the Earth Summit had
been given the opportunity to sign the UN Framework Convention on
Climate Change (1992), which urged industrialized nations to reduce
their emission of greenhouse gases to 1990 levels by 2000. The need
for action was then documented, in 1995, in a report by the Intergovernmental Panel on Climate Change (IPCC), whose work was co-
ordinated by two UN bodies, the UN Environment Program (UNEP)
and the World Meteorological Organization (WMO).

Despite mounting evidence of climate change, some highly developed nations such as the US refused to comply with the 1992 Framework, claiming potential loss of economic growth. To push matters
along, the UN sponsored a meeting in Kyoto, Japan, in December
1997, where major industrialized nations signed a protocol setting hard-and-fast targets for decreasing the emission of six greenhouse gases by more than 5 percent by 2012. The main job now is to
enforce the protocol and persuade skeptics like the US government to
comply.

Meanwhile, the UN has had much more success with another global
climate issue, the ozone hole at the poles. In response to clear scientific evidence that certain manufactured chemicals, especially chloro-
fluorocarbons (CFCs), can catalyze the breakdown of ozone in the
upper atmosphere and thus increase the amount of harmful ultraviolet
sunlight reaching earth, the world community took decisive action
under leadership of UNEP. Under the terms of the 1987 Montreal
Protocol, the industrialized countries banned production of CFCs be-

ginning in 1996, while developing countries were granted a grace period for compliance. All signs indicate that the plans are helping avert an environmental and human catastrophe.

Plants and Animals

We share the biosphere with creatures that are helpless to control human activity and are victims of human folly. We destroy habitat by logging forests and burning prairies or filling in wetlands, and we damage habitat by polluting the air, water, and soil. Plants and animals suffer, including many that we value for their beauty, economic value, or importance in the food chain. The UN Convention on Biological Diversity, signed at the Earth Summit, requires that nations preserve habitats and take other measures to protect plant and animal species. Desertification and deforestation have been identified as major threats to both natural and human habitats. When human misuse turns prairies into desert and forests into acres of denuded soil, all living beings pay the price. Current estimates are that some 900 million people are at risk of losing their livelihood and food supply through desertification. The UN's response is the Convention to Combat Desertification, which entered force in 1996. In the battle to save forests, the Food and Agriculture Organization (FAO), a UN agency, "monitors forest loss and trade in timber and assists developing countries in managing forests."

Plants and animals suffer not only through loss of habitat but through direct human exploitation. Some thirty years ago concern over the growing trade in rare birds, reptiles, fish, and mammals led the UN to create the Convention on International Trade in Endangered Species, which is administered by UNEP. This convention has served as a weapon in the fight against poachers who kill elephants for their tusks, rhinoceroses for their horns, or small mammals for their furs. Fish and fisheries have attracted a great deal of attention in recent decades, owing to a huge increase in the size and effectiveness of commercial fishing fleets, which may be taking fish faster than they can be replaced. The FAO is the world's accepted authority on the

Secretary General Kofi Annan (right, in vehicle) tours Ngorongoro Crater National Park in Tanzania. UN/DPI photo by Milton Grant.

size and exploitation of fish stocks worldwide. In 1995, UN members adopted a legal agreement that would regulate fishing on the high seas, but it has not been ratified by enough nations to make it enforceable.

Now the UN is beginning to deal with yet another human intervention in nature, bioengineering. Advances in cloning promise to alter the living reproductive cycle, while new skills in implanting genes across species make possible the creation of completely new organisms. The potential is vast and unsettling.

Leading UN Actors

Many UN organizations participate in projects or programs that include an environmental aspect: one of them focuses solely on environmental issues.

- The United Nations Environment Program (UNEP), founded in 1972, is based in Nairobi, Kenya. URL: *www.unep.org*

A US government report in 2000 credits UNEP with setting the world's environmental agenda, promoting the environmental dimension of sustainable development, and being an authoritative advocate of the global environment. The US government values its function as a global catalyst of ideas and action and has been UNEP's biggest donor from the beginning. The US government was especially impressed by UNEP's success in concluding the Stockholm Convention on Persistent Organic Pollutants, which regulates potentially hazardous chemicals that are no longer commonly used in the US but remain in the environment and the food chain for a long time and can be transported long distances by water and wind.

- The United Nations Educational, Scientific, and Cultural Organization (UNESCO), founded in 1946, is based in Paris, France. URL: www.unesco.org

UNESCO has a varied mission involving education, research, and public outreach in the sciences, culture, and communications. With 188 member states and a staff of 2,000, it includes 178 national commissions and some 5,000 UNESCO associations, centers, and clubs. The budget for 2000–2001 was $544 million. In 1984, the US withdrew from UNESCO owing to policy differences but retained official observer status and is likely to rejoin soon. In 2000, the US government gave $2.25 million in voluntary contribution to UNESCO programs for the free flow of ideas, open access to education, the transfer of scientific knowledge, and protection of cultural and natural heritages.

- The World Meteorological Organization (WMO), founded in 1951, is based in Geneva, Switzerland. URL: www.wmo.ch

The WMO is a specialized agency that provides current scientific information about the atmosphere, freshwaters, and climate. Depletion of the ozone layer, global warming, floods and droughts, and El Niño are among the concerns it addresses. Its staff of 246 serves 179 member states and 6 territories. Its budget for 2000–2003 was $152 million.

CHAPTER 23

UN to the Rescue

The usual face of the UN in the most difficult spots today is not the face of peacekeepers. It's the face of the World Food Program person, it's the face of the refugee person, it's the face of the UNICEF person.

—Carol Bellamy, Director of UNICEF

The UN has always regarded disaster aid as one of its primary missions, defining "disaster" in broad terms that range from earthquakes and floods to disease and famine. Humanitarian aid organizations operate in collaboration with the UN Emergency Relief Coordinator and a committee of representatives from UN agencies and major nongovernmental organizations like the Red Cross.

Which body of the UN responds to a given emergency depends on the nature of the situation. If food and shelter are needed, the World Food Program might be the lead agency. Although the WFP engages in social and economic development, its main focus is on helping victims of disaster, long-term refugees, and displaced persons. In 2000, the program's full-time staff of 2,355 fed almost 90 million people in more than 80 nations. The WFP is the largest UN provider of grant assistance to Africa, and it provided vital food supplies in

A young Somali mother and her children
await medical treatment at a UNICEF/
Swede relief clinic. UN photo 159385 by
Milton Grant.

2000 to the Horn of Africa, North Korea, the Balkans, Afghanistan,
the former Soviet Union and Eastern Europe, and Latin America and
the Caribbean, particularly Haiti, Nicaragua, Bolivia, and Honduras.

Often the WFP collaborates with other UN bodies, such as the High
Commissioner for Refugees (UNHCR) or the UN Children's Fund
(UNICEF), and with NGOs that help distribute aid and ensure that it
goes where most needed. The UNHCR is charged with helping and
protecting refugees, fulfilling this mission so successfully that it received Nobel Peace Prizes in 1954 and 1981. It has developed "quick
impact projects," or QIPs, to bridge the gap between emergency assistance for refugees and for refugees returning home and longer-term

development aid undertaken by other agencies. Typical QIPs rebuild
schools, repair roads, or restore water supplies. Media coverage has
made the UNHCR's blue plastic tents familiar to Americans as they
view events in Kosovo, West Africa, and elsewhere.

UNICEF looks after children in need. Its main task is to help children in developing countries achieve their full potential as human
beings, which it does by focusing on rights, needs, and opportunities.
Its bedrock statement of belief is the Convention on the Rights of the
Child (CRC), ratified by all the world's nations (except the United
States and Somalia, which are expected to ratify it soon), which lays
out a kind of Bill of Rights for children. The convention expresses
a rights-based approach that encourages governments to adopt internationally recognized ethical standards and to go beyond minimal
assurances that citizens have the basics to survive. UNICEF addresses
children's needs through research and information programs, partnerships with governments and NGOs for provision of vital services,
and emergency operations. And it addresses opportunities for children by working with governments and other organizations to ensure
good medical care and upbringing.

Leading UN Actors

Four organizations are preeminent in the UN's relief efforts:

- The World Food Program (WFP), created in 1963, is headquartered
  in Rome, Italy. URL: *www.wfp.org*
  The WFP underwent a major administrative reformation under
  Catherine Bertini, the organization's first American and first
  woman Executive Director. A recent US government report praised
  her internal reforms and noted that "significantly, the WFP has the
  largest budget, the smallest staff, and the lowest percentage of administrative costs within the UN system." In fiscal 2000, the US was
  the WFP's biggest benefactor, contributing $795.7 million of its
  $1.685 billion budget.
- The Office of the United Nations High Commissioner for Refugees

New residents arrive at the Rogani refugee camp in Chaman, a Pakistani border town where children and young people make up a large portion of the population. UN/DPI photo by Luke Powell.

(UNHCR), established in 1950, is based in Geneva, Switzerland. URL: *www.unhcr.ch*

The UNHCR publishes a biennial report on the status of the world's refugees. A staff of about 5,000 works in 281 offices in 121 countries and looks after 21.6 million people. In 2000, operations were concentrated in western Asia (some 2.6 million Afghan refugees), the former Yugoslavia, and the Great Lakes region of Africa. Almost all of the $965.2 million budget came from voluntary donations from governments.

• The United Nations Children's Fund (UNICEF), founded in 1946, is headquartered in New York City. URL: *www.unicef.org*

UNICEF has become embedded in the American consciousness through its famous holiday cards. The organization has 8 regional offices and 126 country offices, a staff of 9,000, and an annual budget of $1.2 billion. Its director since 1995 is Carol Bellamy, formerly president of the New York City Council. The US government has invariably been UNICEF's largest single donor.

- The UN Relief and Works Agency for Palestine Refugees in the Near East (UNRWA), founded in 1949, is based in Gaza City, Palestine. URL: *www.unrwa.org*

  Founded to provide emergency humanitarian aid to Palestinians displaced during the creation of the state of Israel, the UNRWA has become a permanent social services agency. It provides health, education, and social services to more than 3.6 million registered Palestinian refugees in the Middle East, under the eye of a UN Coordinator. The US government has usually been the largest donor, contributing $101 million in 2000.

CHAPTER 24

Nuclear, Biological, and Chemical Threats

We need a reaffirmation of political commitment to reduce the dangers from existing nuclear weapons and from further proliferation.
—Kofi Annan, Secretary General of the UN

Building homes on old chemical dumps like Love Canal or sending anthrax spores through the mail may seem like plots from bad movies. Unfortunately, the bad movies are getting a second showing in the theater of real life. Today, there are even scarier plots, involving deadly nerve gas and nuclear weapons smuggled into urban centers and airports. The UN's global presence makes it a natural leader in identifying and monitoring these dangers and confining them so they harm no one.

The UN has long been a forum for talks about arms control and disarmament, and some of these discussions have produced solid results. UN-sponsored or related negotiations have led to such major agreements as the Nuclear Non-Proliferation Treaty (1968), the Comprehensive Nuclear-Test-Ban Treaty (1996), and treaties outlawing chemical (1992) and bacteriological weapons (1972) and the placement of nuclear weapons on the seabed (1971) or in outer space (1967).

Equally important, the UN has helped establish methods to control weapons of mass destruction. The International Atomic Energy Agency (IAEA), for example, has set up a system of nuclear safeguards and verification, and the Organization for the Prohibition of Chemical Weapons (OPCW) monitors compliance with the Convention on Chemical Weapons.

One of the more insidious weapons of war is the land mine, a small explosive device that can be buried in the ground, where it explodes with deadly force when stepped on. Cheap and easy to deploy, land mines have proliferated in all kinds of conflicts, even civil wars, where they become silent killers. Even worse, when hostilities end, a mine typically remains buried in the ground, often forgotten until some innocent person steps on it and loses a leg or worse. It is estimated that each year some 2 million mines are laid worldwide, and during that year they kill and wound more than 20,000 people. The UN is credited with encouraging countries to support the 1997 Ottawa Convention, which bans the production, export, and use of land mines. The UN operates mine clearance projects in seven countries and also trains de-miners. It offers public education programs and improves medical and rehabilitation services for land mine victims.

Leading UN Actors

Of the three UN bodies responsible for overseeing nuclear, biological, or chemical threats, the IAEA is best known to the public, owing to its monitoring of the nuclear arms potential of Iran and North Korea.

• The International Atomic Agency (IAEA), established in 1957, is based in Vienna, Austria. URL: *www.iaea.org*

   The IAEA is an independent intergovernmental agency that helps coordinate the fields of nuclear science and engineering and eases the transfer of technology among nations. Safety and the protection of people against excessive exposure to radiation have been important concerns as well. The organization is probably best known as the watchdog for international treaties aimed at containing the unauthorized spread or distribution of nuclear weapons or materials. Its inspectors watch more than a thousand nuclear installations worldwide that are covered under the IAEA Safeguards Program. The US government strongly endorses the work of the agency and provides more than one quarter of the $300 million annual cost. In the aftermath of the attack on the US on Sept. 11, 2001, the IAEA has become a leader in the debate about preventing terrorists from using nuclear weapons.

- The Organization for the Prohibition of Chemical Weapons (OPCW) is headquartered at The Hague, Netherlands. URL: *www.opcw.org*

  The primary task of the OPCW is to monitor the provisions of the 1972 Convention on the Prohibition of the Development, Production, and Stockpiling of Bacteriological (Biological) and Toxin Weapons and on Their Destruction and the Convention on the Prohibition of the Development, Production, Stockpiling, and Use of Chemical Weapons and on Their Destruction.

- The Preparatory Commission for the Comprehensive Nuclear-Test-Ban Treaty Organization (CTBTO), established in 1996, is based in Vienna, Austria. URL: *www.ctbto.org*

  The commission's main job is to devise a verification plan to ensure that the signers of the Nuclear-Test-Ban Treaty are adhering to its terms.

CHAPTER 25

Guiding Globalization: How the
UN Helps Make Things Work

The surest route to growth is through successfully engaging in the global economy, combined with effective social policies.

—Kofi Annan, Secretary General of the United Nations

Free markets work best when they have strong government underpinnings, but no one government is in charge of global markets. This is where the UN has become invaluable as the monitor, administrator, and facilitator of the many "soft infrastructures" that enable complex international financial and industrial markets to work reasonably well most of the time. The UN has also provided vital aid to governments trying to cope with the fast pace and intensity of modern economic relations, including the rapid swings in currency and capital that can send a seemingly sound national economy into sudden crisis.

Capital Opportunities

The smooth flow of capital is crucial for market systems, and here the UN has been a key player on both modest and global scales. A modest example is the recent collaborative efforts between the UN Conference on Trade and Development (UNCTAD) and the International Chamber of Commerce, which are compiling investment guides to the forty-eight least developed countries as a way of publicizing opportunities and encouraging capital inflows. Some thirty companies are participating in a pilot venture in six countries. Another example is UNCTAD's joint effort with information technology companies to develop an automated customs system that has been implemented in more than seventy developing countries.

Far bigger and better known is the work of the International Monetary Fund (IMF), a specialized agency that offers capital, fiscal and monetary advice, and policy recommendations to national governments. Unlike the World Bank, the IMF's writ runs to all nations, not just the developing ones. Most of its work proceeds quietly and consists of complex services aimed at easing international monetary cooperation, establishing a multilateral system of payments, eliminating foreign exchange restrictions, and promoting stable and orderly exchange rates. In times of crisis, when a member nation is unable to meet its foreign obligations or its financial system becomes unstable, the IMF can offer essential aid in the form of large loans. However, the loans often come bound with strings of fiscal reform that some nations find difficult to untie. The IMF's insistence, for example, that Indonesia and other developing countries cut their government spending as part of receiving bailout loans is cited by some as a contributing factor to the Asian economic collapse of the late 1990s. The IMF has conceded that it may have acted with undue severity and has reexamined its policies.

Soft Infrastructure

For every piece of machinery, every length of fiber-optic cable, every chemical reagent, there has to be a technical standard that permits the enforcement of consistency and standardization. UN bodies set technical standards for machines and the like, and also for laws, procedures, and other intangible elements of the infrastructure.

Another kind of soft infrastructure is the individual capacity to acquire and process information. The UN Secretary General has spoken often about the importance of information access as a basis for economic and social improvement. Alluding to the "digital divide" that helps separate the affluent from the poor nations, Kofi Annan has proposed that the UN should begin targeting specific information needs through its programs. In 2001 he announced the creation of the Health InterNetwork, which will have 10,000 on-site electronic information access locations in hospitals, clinics, and public health facilities throughout the developing world. The World Health Organization is the lead agency in this effort to bring the latest medical information to literally billions of people.

Soft infrastructure also includes the rules and standards for the creation, ownership, and development of intellectual property. Software, songs, and genes can all be regarded as forms of property that have value. And as with any form of property, disputes arise about ownership and use. The UN has a specialized agency that deals with exactly these kinds of concerns. The World Intellectual Property Organization (WIPO) provides services such as helping nations harmonize their laws and procedures about intellectual property, so that creators in each country can more easily be protected in other countries. WIPO also develops common international standards and procedures regarding issues like patents, copyrights, and trademarks. It administers eleven treaties that set out internationally agreed rights and common standards, which the signatory states agree to enforce within their own borders. The Internet, digitization, and e-commerce have made WIPO even more important by raising basic issues of the right to copy and use intellectual property, especially music and films. WIPO has developed global registration systems for trademarks, industrial designs, and other intellectual property. The Patent Cooperation Treaty (PCT), for example, establishes a single international patent that has legal force in signatory nations. WIPO provides another vital service, helping inventors determine whether their invention is truly new. Anyone who applies for a patent in their home country must show that their idea is new and that no one else owns it. The search for this kind of information can involve a vast amount of work, so WIPO has simplified matters by creating a classification system that organizes information pertaining to inventions, trademarks, and industrial designs into indexed structures for easy retrieval. The system defines about 70,000 technology categories, grouped under major headings such as biotechnology and medicines.

Global Compact

One of the more ingenious ideas at the UN has been to engage the business community in a common effort to act according to internationally accepted standards, such as treaties against child labor. Kofi Annan proposed the Global Compact, as he dubbed it, at the 1999 World Economic Forum in Davos, Switzerland. He challenged the business community to accept and enforce a set of core values in the areas of human rights, labor standards, and environmental practices. Annan asked them to:

Respect the protection of international human rights
Check to be sure they are not committing or abetting human rights abuses
Support freedom of association and the right to unionize
Eliminate forced and child labor
Eliminate occupational discrimination
Be more environmentally responsible and responsive

If businesses do this globally, the UN's agenda would advance substantially, without the need to create more bureaucracy or laws. It is an elegant approach, certainly worth trying. In response, the International Chamber of Commerce formally accepted Annan's challenge on behalf of its 7,000 business organizations in 137 nations. The Global Compact is now operating as a grand experiment in advancing the UN's agenda through cooperation rather than the traditional mechanisms of censure and sanctions.

Leading UN Actors

The following organizations are among those that facilitate globalization.

- The International Monetary Fund (IMF), established in 1944 at the Bretton Woods Conference, is based in Washington, D.C. URL: *www.imf.int*

    The IMF facilitates international monetary cooperation and provides loans to member states. The 182 member nations are each represented on the board of governors, which sets policy and has general oversight. Regular operations are managed by a twenty-four-member executive board. Member countries subscribe to the IMF through contributions to the budget, and can draw on IMF loans according to the level of their subscription. The IMF publishes two important reports: *World Economic Outlook* and *International Capital Markets*.

- The World Intellectual Property Organization (WIPO) was founded in 1970 and became a UN specialized agency in 1974. It is based in Geneva, Switzerland. URL: *www.wipo.int*

    WIPO's mission is to help protect intellectual property worldwide. Its annual budget is 410 million Swiss francs, 85 percent of which it raises through earnings from registration systems.

- The International Civil Aviation Organization (ICAO) was created in 1944, has been a UN specialized agency since 1947, and is based in Montreal, Canada. URL: *www.icao.int*

    ICAO sets the international standards and regulations necessary for the safety and efficiency of air transport. It does this by establishing international standards for aircraft, pilots and flight crews, air traffic controllers, ground and maintenance crews, and security in international airports. It is also concerned with flight rules and telecommunications systems. At a 2002 ICAO ministerial conference on anti-terrorism airline regulations, attendees agreed on a security plan that includes audits of airport security. The US, a strong supporter of the ICAO, provided one quarter of its $52.58 million budget for 2000.

- The International Maritime Organization (IMO), founded in 1959, is headquartered in London, England. URL: *www.imo.org*

    The IMO's mandate is to make the process of shipping goods for international trade safer and less likely to pollute the seas. Through

its meetings, 40 conventions, and 800 codes and recommendations, the IMO has helped develop common standards of safety
and efficiency in navigation, technical regulations and practices,
and pollution control. The IMO founded the World Maritime University in 1983 in Sweden and has also established the IMO International Maritime Law Institute and the IMO International Maritime Academy.

- The International Telecommunication Union (ITU), founded in
  1865 in Paris as the International Telegraph Union, became the
  ITU in 1934. It became a UN specialized agency in 1947 and is
  located in Geneva, Switzerland. URL: *www.itu.int*

  The ITU helps government and the private sector coordinate
  and improve global telecommunication networks and services. The
  staff of some 740 also offers technical assistance to developing
  countries.

- The Universal Postal Union (UPU), established in the Berne Treaty
  of 1874, became a UN specialized agency in 1948. It is headquartered in Berne, Switzerland. URL: *www.upu.int*

  The UPU regulates and facilitates cooperation among international postal services, as well as providing advice, mediation, and
  technical assistance. The Universal Postal Congress meets every
  five years.

CHAPTER 26

Drug Trafficking

Drug abuse is a global phenomenon. It affects almost every country although its extent and characteristics differ from region to region. Drug abuse trends around the world, especially among youth, have started to converge over the last few decades. —UN Office on Drugs and Crime

A downside of globalization has been the spread of international organized crime, often centered around the illegal trade of drugs, weapons, or humans. Crime is an abridgment of human rights. The mugger who steals a man's wallet has abridged his rights to security of person and property. The computer hacker who steals personal financial information abridges a woman's right to privacy. And perhaps most insidious and destructive of all is the combination of criminal activity and drug addiction. The drug lords who supply cocaine, heroine, Ecstasy, and other substances diminish the human capacity for independent living, often subverting local law enforcement through bribery. The drug trade has recently become even more ominous through its connections with international terrorism.

The UN Response

The rapid growth of the international narcotics trade has led the UN to streamline and better coordinate its anti-drug resources under the Office on Drugs and Crime (UNODC), established in 1997. The office consists of two parts: the Crime Program (discussed in Chapter 8) and the Drug Program, formally known as the UN Drug Control Program (UNDCP). Through the Drug Program, the UNODC offers an integrated approach that begins with the farmer and ends with the drug dealer and money launderer. The UNDCP also monitors implementation of drug-related decisions by ECOSOC and other UN bodies.

The governing body of the UNDCP is the Commission on Narcotic Drugs (CND), a functional commission of ECOSOC and the UN's main source of drug-related policy. Three international conventions form the basis for the CND's policies: the Single Convention on Narcotic Drugs (1961), which tries to confine drugs to medical use only; the Convention on Psychotropic Substances (1971), which seeks to control synthetic drugs; and the UN Convention against Illicit Traffic in Narcotic Drugs and Psychotropic Substances (1988), which deals mainly with drug trafficking and related issues like money laundering. However, the CND does not actually monitor implementation of these treaties. That task is the responsibility of the International Narcotics Control Board (INCB), an independent panel of 13 persons elected by ECOSOC and financed by the UN.

Among the UNODC's major efforts are the Global Assessment Program (GAP), which provides accurate information about the international drug problem; the legal Advisory Program, which assists governments in writing laws against the drug trade and helps train judicial officials; and the Illicit Crop Monitoring Program (ICMP), whose projects in six major drug-growing countries (Afghanistan, Bolivia, Colombia, Laos, Myanmar, and Peru) aim at discovering the extent and nature of drug crops such as coca bush and opium poppy. The Alternative Development Program tries to nip the drug problem at its source by offering farmers alternative crops that will enable them to earn a decent, and legal, living. This approach is being tested through projects in Latin America, Southwest Asia, and Southeast Asia.

The UNDCP encourages the cultivation of alternative crops to replace opium poppy, as on this farm in Thailand. UN/DPI photo by J. Sailas/UNDCP.

The UN's drug experts are becoming increasingly concerned about changing perceptions of drugs among youth. If our future lies with young people, we need to pay attention to the relation between youth and drugs. Things change, and old approaches may no longer work. That was the message the director of the UNDCP's youth programs delivered at a conference in 2002. He noted that young people are increasingly drawn toward synthetic drugs rather than those, like heroin, derived from poppies and other biological organisms. Such drugs are worse, in some ways, he claimed, because although they usually don't cause physical dependence and the painful withdrawal symptoms associated with heroin use, they do cause lasting and irreversible physical and neurological damage that may not become manifest until later in life. As the director observed, most young people who use Ecstasy think of it not as doing drugs, but merely as having a good time. Intervention or advice from adults usually doesn't work because of the generation gap, so the alternative is to encourage peer-to-peer education. Accordingly, UN narcotics experts are considering methods for reshaping their programs to include more youth as role models.

The Connection with Terrorism

Many reports in recent years have shown that some terrorist organizations rely on the drug trade to raise money for their operations. Ob-
viously, any dent in the narcotics trade may therefore also help combat
terrorism, but a more focused approach would have an even greater
impact. One UN plan has been to identify the nations that are the
largest producers of opium and strongly encourage them to take action. That has put the spotlight on Afghanistan, which has been the
world's largest opium producer in most recent years.

The UN and the US leaned hard on the former Taliban regime to
stop the growing of poppies, which had become virtually the basis of
the national economy. They succeeded, and as Afghanistan's output
rapidly declined, the distinction of being the global opium capital
moved to Myanmar (formerly Burma). However, experts also began
noticing that the Afghan drug networks were stockpiling much of the
opium and processed heroin rather than destroying it, which meant
that a large supply was available to anyone who could control it, including the Taliban regime. And because the Taliban and the Al Qaeda
terrorist network had become virtually synonymous, it did not take
much imagination to see how drug money could become terrorist
funding.

When the US and its allies intervened in Afghanistan in late 2001,
the Taliban ended its controls over poppy growing, and, predictably,
the supply of opium in the region began rising. The collapse of the
Taliban regime in winter 2001 enabled farmers to act with impunity
and begin planting as much acreage in poppies as they could manage,
an absolutely alarming thought to the European nations, who had
been inundated with Afghan opium in previous years. At meetings
sponsored by the Commission on Narcotic Drugs in Europe and
Japan, experts warned that Afghanistan was poised to regain its pre-
mier status as an opium producer. The new Afghan government has
committed itself to a strong anti-drug, anti-poppy-growing policy, although it is uncertain if it can carry this out. Afghan's farmers have
few options in their choice of cash crops, and opium heads the list for

profit per unit of investment and ease of transport along the country's bad roads. If the new government acts too harshly it will alienate some of its supporters, and if it moves too slowly it will anger the US and its allies. But finding an alternative crop will not be easy, and making the changeover on the farms will require investment capital that the government doesn't have.

A lot is riding on success. An agricultural system based on legal crops would enable the nation to prosper and participate fully in the international community. Yet the return of poppy cultivation would inevitably bring organized crime, official corruption, and possibly links with terrorist organizations. All the world's nations have an interest in the fate of Afghanistan's poppy fields, and the UN has begun aligning its bodies to act effectively. Among other things, the UN has reestablished its UNDCP Afghanistan office.

Leading UN Actors

Three bodies oversee most of the UN's fight against the trade in illegal drugs.

- The UN Office on Drugs and Crime (UNODC), established in 1997, is based in Vienna, Austria. URL: *www.unodc.org*

    The UNODC has two components, the Crime Program and the Drug Program. The Crime Program focuses on corruption, organized crime, trafficking in human beings, and terrorism. The Drug Program compiles and disseminates information about illicit drugs, monitors illegal drug-related agriculture, fights the laundering of drug-related money, seeks alternative crops for farmers in drug-growing regions, and helps governments write anti-drug legislation. The UNODC has some 350 staff and 22 field offices. Most of its funding comes from voluntary contributions by member states.

- The Commission on Narcotic Drugs (CND) was established in 1946 and has its headquarters in Vienna, Austria. URL: *www. uncnd.org*

    The CND makes UN policy about drugs and is the governing

body for the UN Drug Control Program (UNDCP). It is a functional commission of ECOSOC.

- The International Narcotics Control Board (INCB) was created in 1968 and is located in Vienna, Austria. *www.incb.org*

The INCB is an independent body, funded by the UN, that monitors compliance with the three international conventions on narcotics and drug trafficking.

Conclusion

The campaign to end Afghanistan's opium industry offers powerful evidence that the UN is a deadly serious organization. For most Americans, who have little direct interaction with the world organization, it is easy to think that the UN's main value and mission lie far away. And often they do. Yet in our interconnected world, far away may also be right next door, as the terrorist attacks of September 11, 2001, demonstrated with brutal force. A prudent person must conclude that global safety and security come from many sources, in many ways, and that whatever the awesome power of the US, it should not, and need not, march alone.

By the same token, the UN cannot succeed without the US. We have seen that the UN has a tremendous mandate, greater than that of any other organization—even its predecessor, the ill-fated League of Nations (to which the US never belonged). The UN, by itself, lacks the resources to fulfill much of its mandate, and its partners—the nations of Europe, Asia, Africa, and the Americas—cannot act with unity of purpose and with the material resources available to the US.

The attacks of 9/11 have jolted both the UN and the US into seriously redefining their historic relationship. The current Secretary General, as we have seen, understands the mutual interests and needs of the two and seems to realize that he has a rare opportunity to reinvent their relationship. The US government, for its part, now has a clear basis for its foreign and domestic policy in the form of international terrorism, which has replaced the Soviet Union, the "evil empire" of cold war days, as the major external threat to the nation. Perhaps as a result, Americans may replace the consumerism and market-economy rhetoric of the acquisitive 1990s with moral and psychological clarity. That focus could make the US a much more effective player at the UN, where, as our insiders have noted, the American government generally gets what it wants when it knows what it wants, but flounders when it is uncertain about its policies or goals.

Something to Think About

"I'm struck by the relevance of the UN to United States foreign policy and national security interests. If you look at the agenda that we've had since I've been here, it very much tracks with the agenda of our foreign policy and of our national security policy. To those who would question the relevance of the UN, my answer would be: absolutely the UN is relevant, no question about it, all you have to do is look at our agenda. The degree of UN involvement in any specific issue will vary from case to case, but there will always be a UN role. The debate is going to be over the precise definition of that role, and it seems to vary from situation to situation."   —John Negroponte, US Ambassador to the UN

Will the UN be capable of delivering on its end of the bargain? Partly that depends on how much it promises to offer, and how much the US expects. The UN, remember, is not a government but rather a creature of the world's governments, and is constrained by severe limits on its ability to raise money and impose its decisions. It is therefore vital that US legislators and policy makers, as well as the general public, understand how the UN is constituted and, even more important, how it functions—not just on a flowchart but in real life and real time. If it is true, as French statesman Georges Clemenceau once said, that war is too important to be left to the generals, the UN and its relationship with the US are too important to be left solely to the experts.

Membership of Principal United Nations Organs in 2002

GENERAL ASSEMBLY

The General Assembly is composed of all 191 United Nations Member States.

The States, and the dates on which they became members, are listed in Appendix C.

SECURITY COUNCIL

The Security Council has 15 members. The United Nations Charter designates five states as permanent members and the General Assembly elects 10 other members for two-year terms. The term of office for each nonpermanent member of the Council ends on 31 December of the year indicated in parentheses next to its name.

The five permanent members of the Security Council are China, France, Russian Federation, United Kingdom, and the United States.

The 10 nonpermanent members of the Council in 2002 are Bulgaria (2003), Cameroon (2003), Colombia (2002), Guinea (2003), Ireland (2002), Mauritius (2002), Mexico (2003), Norway (2002), Singapore (2002), and Syria (2003).

ECONOMIC AND SOCIAL COUNCIL

The Economic and Social Council has 54 members, elected for three-year terms by the General Assembly. The term of office for each member expires on 31 December of the year indicated in parentheses next to its name. In 2002, the Council is composed of the following 54 States:

Andorra (2003), Angola (2002), Argentina (2003), Australia (2004), Austria (2002), Bahrain (2002), Benin (2002), Bhutan (2004), Brazil (2003), Burkina Faso (2002), Burundi (2004), Cameroon (2002), Chile (2004), China (2004), Costa Rica (2002), Croatia (2002), Cuba (2002), Egypt (2003), El Salvador (2004), Ethiopia (2003), Fiji (2002), Finland (2004), France (2002), Georgia (2003), Germany (2002), Ghana (2004), Greece (2002), Guatemala (2004), Hungary (2004), India (2004), Iran (2003), Italy (2003), Japan (2002), Libya (2004), Mexico (2002), Nepal (2003), Netherlands (2003), Nigeria (2003), Pakistan (2003), Peru (2003), Portugal (2002), Qatar (2004), Republic of Korea (2003), Romania (2003), Russian Federation (2004), South Africa (2003), Sudan (2002), Suriname (2002), Sweden (2004), Uganda (2003), Ukraine (2004), United Kingdom (2004), United States (2003), and Zimbabwe (2004).

TRUSTEESHIP COUNCIL

The Trusteeship Council is made up of the five permanent members of the Security Council—China, France, Russian Federation, United Kingdom, and the United States. With the independence of Palau, the last remaining United Nations Trust Territory, the Council formally suspended operations on 1 November 1994. The Council amended its rules of procedure to drop the obligation to meet annually and agreed to meet as the occasion required; by its decision or the decision of its President or at the request of a majority of its members or the General Assembly or the Security Council.

INTERNATIONAL COURT OF JUSTICE

The International Court of Justice has 15 members, elected by both the General Assembly and the Security Council. Judges hold nine-year terms, which end 5 February of the year indicated in parentheses next to their name.

The current composition of the Court is as follows: Awn Shawkat Al-Khasawneh (Jordan) (2009); Nabil Elaraby (Egypt) (2006); Thomas Buergenthal (United States) (2006); Carl-August Fleischhauer (Germany) (2003); Gilbert Guillaume (France) (2009); Géza Herczegh (Hungary) (2003); Rosalyn Higgins (United Kingdom) (2009); Shi Jiuyong (China) (2003); Pieter H. Kooijmans (Netherlands) (2006); Abdul G. Koroma (Sierra Leone) (2003); Shigeru Oda (Japan) (2003); Gonzalo Parra-Aranguren (Venezuela) (2009); Raymond Ranjeva (Madagascar) (2009); José Francisco Rezek (Brazil) (2006); and Vladlen S. Vereshchetin (Russian Federation) (2006).

Universal Declaration of Human Rights

PREAMBLE

Whereas recognition of the inherent dignity and of the equal and inalienable rights of all members of the human family is the foundation of freedom, justice and peace in the world,

Whereas disregard and contempt for human rights have resulted in barbarous acts which have outraged the conscience of mankind, and the advent of a world in which human beings shall enjoy freedom of speech and belief and freedom from fear and want has been proclaimed as the highest aspiration of the common people,

Whereas it is essential, if man is not to be compelled to have recourse, as a last resort, to rebellion against tyranny and oppression, that human rights should be protected by the rule of law,

Whereas it is essential to promote the development of friendly relations between nations,

Whereas the peoples of the United Nations have in the Charter reaffirmed their faith in fundamental human rights, in the dignity and worth of the human person and in the equal rights of men and women and have determined to promote social progress and better standards of life in larger freedom,

Whereas Member States have pledged themselves to achieve, in co-operation with the United Nations, the promotion of universal respect for and observance of human rights and fundamental freedoms,

Whereas a common understanding of these rights and freedoms is of the greatest importance for the full realization of this pledge,

Now, Therefore THE GENERAL ASSEMBLY proclaims THIS UNIVERSAL DECLARATION OF HUMAN RIGHTS as a common standard of achievement for all peoples and all nations, to the end that every individual and every organ of society, keeping this Declaration constantly in mind, shall strive by teaching and education to promote respect for these rights and freedoms and by progressive measures, national and international, to secure their universal and effective recognition and observance, both among the peoples of Member States themselves and among the peoples of territories under their jurisdiction.

Article 1.
All human beings are born free and equal in dignity and rights. They are endowed with reason and conscience and should act towards one another in a spirit of brotherhood.

Article 2.
Everyone is entitled to all the rights and freedoms set forth in this Declaration, without distinction of any kind, such as race, colour, sex, language, religion, political or other opinion, national or social origin, property, birth or other status. Furthermore, no distinction shall be made on the basis of the political, jurisdictional or international status of the country or territory to which a person belongs, whether it be independent, trust, non-self-governing or under any other limitation of sovereignty.

Article 3.
Everyone has the right to life, liberty and security of person.

Article 4.
No one shall be held in slavery or servitude; slavery and the slave trade shall be prohibited in all their forms.

Article 5.
No one shall be subjected to torture or to cruel, inhuman or degrading treatment or punishment.

Article 6.
Everyone has the right to recognition everywhere as a person before the law.

Article 7.
All are equal before the law and are entitled without any discrimination to equal protection of the law. All are entitled to equal protection against any discrimination in violation of this Declaration and against any incitement to such discrimination.

Article 8.
Everyone has the right to an effective remedy by the competent national tribunals for acts violating the fundamental rights granted him by the constitution or by law.

Article 9.
No one shall be subjected to arbitrary arrest, detention or exile.

Article 10.
Everyone is entitled in full equality to a fair and public hearing by an independent and impartial tribunal, in the determination of his rights and obligations and of any criminal charge against him.

Article 11.
(1) Everyone charged with a penal offence has the right to be presumed innocent until proved guilty according to law in a public trial at which he has had all the guarantees necessary for his defence.
(2) No one shall be held guilty of any penal offence on account of any act or omission which did not constitute a penal offence, under

national or international law, at the time when it was committed. Nor shall a heavier penalty be imposed than the one that was applicable at the time the penal offence was committed.

Article 12.

No one shall be subjected to arbitrary interference with his privacy, family, home or correspondence, nor to attacks upon his honour and reputation. Everyone has the right to the protection of the law against such interference or attacks.

Article 13.

(1) Everyone has the right to freedom of movement and residence within the borders of each state.

(2) Everyone has the right to leave any country, including his own, and to return to his country.

Article 14.

(1) Everyone has the right to seek and to enjoy in other countries asylum from persecution.

(2) This right may not be invoked in the case of prosecutions genuinely arising from non-political crimes or from acts contrary to the purposes and principles of the United Nations.

Article 15.

(1) Everyone has the right to a nationality.

(2) No one shall be arbitrarily deprived of his nationality nor denied the right to change his nationality.

Article 16.

(1) Men and women of full age, without any limitation due to race, nationality or religion, have the right to marry and to found a family. They are entitled to equal rights as to marriage, during marriage and at its dissolution.

(2) Marriage shall be entered into only with the free and full consent of the intending spouses.

(3) The family is the natural and fundamental group unit of society and is entitled to protection by society and the State.

Article 17.

(1) Everyone has the right to own property alone as well as in association with others.

(2) No one shall be arbitrarily deprived of his property.

Article 18.

Everyone has the right to freedom of thought, conscience and religion; this right includes freedom to change his religion or belief, and freedom, either alone or in community with others and in public or private, to manifest his religion or belief in teaching, practice, worship and observance.

Article 19.

Everyone has the right to freedom of opinion and expression; this right includes freedom to hold opinions without interference and to seek, receive and impart information and ideas through any media and regardless of frontiers.

Article 20.

(1) Everyone has the right to freedom of peaceful assembly and association.

(2) No one may be compelled to belong to an association.

Article 21.

(1) Everyone has the right to take part in the government of his country, directly or through freely chosen representatives.

(2) Everyone has the right of equal access to public service in his country.

(3) The will of the people shall be the basis of the authority of government; this will shall be expressed in periodic and genuine elections which shall be by universal and equal suffrage and shall be held by secret vote or by equivalent free voting procedures.

Article 22.

Everyone, as a member of society, has the right to social security and is entitled to realization, through national effort and international co-operation and in accordance with the organization and resources of each State, of the economic, social and cultural rights indispensable for his dignity and the free development of his personality.

Article 23.

(1) Everyone has the right to work, to free choice of employment, to just and favourable conditions of work and to protection against unemployment.

(2) Everyone, without any discrimination, has the right to equal pay for equal work.

(3) Everyone who works has the right to just and favourable remuneration ensuring for himself and his family an existence worthy of human dignity, and supplemented, if necessary, by other means of social protection.

(4) Everyone has the right to form and to join trade unions for the protection of his interests.

Article 24.

Everyone has the right to rest and leisure, including reasonable limitation of working hours and periodic holidays with pay.

Article 25.

(1) Everyone has the right to a standard of living adequate for the health and well-being of himself and of his family, including food, clothing, housing and medical care and necessary social services, and the right to security in the event of unemployment, sickness, disability, widowhood, old age or other lack of livelihood in circumstances beyond his control.

(2) Motherhood and childhood are entitled to special care and assistance. All children, whether born in or out of wedlock, shall enjoy the same social protection.

Article 26.

(1) Everyone has the right to education. Education shall be free, at least in the elementary and fundamental stages. Elementary education shall be compulsory. Technical and professional education shall be made generally available and higher education shall be equally accessible to all on the basis of merit.

(2) Education shall be directed to the full development of the human personality and to the strengthening of respect for human rights and fundamental freedoms. It shall promote understanding, tolerance and friendship among all nations, racial or religious groups, and shall further the activities of the United Nations for the maintenance of peace.

(3) Parents have a prior right to choose the kind of education that shall be given to their children.

Article 27.

(1) Everyone has the right freely to participate in the cultural life of the community, to enjoy the arts and to share in scientific advancement and its benefits.

(2) Everyone has the right to the protection of the moral and material interests resulting from any scientific, literary or artistic production of which he is the author.

Article 28.

Everyone is entitled to a social and international order in which the rights and freedoms set forth in this Declaration can be fully realized.

Article 29.

(1) Everyone has duties to the community in which alone the free and full development of his personality is possible.

(2) In the exercise of his rights and freedoms, everyone shall be subject only to such limitations as are determined by law solely for the purpose of securing due recognition and respect for the rights and freedoms of others and of meeting the just requirements of morality, public order and the general welfare in a democratic society.

(3) These rights and freedoms may in no case be exercised contrary to the purposes and principles of the United Nations.

Article 30.

Nothing in this Declaration may be interpreted as implying for any State, group or person any right to engage in any activity or to perform any act aimed at the destruction of any of the rights and freedoms set forth herein.

UN Member States

The 191 member states, with the date on which each joined the United Nations:

Afghanistan   Nov. 19, 1946
Albania   Dec. 14, 1955
Algeria   Oct. 8, 1962
Andorra   July 28, 1993
Angola   Dec. 1, 1976
Antigua and Barbuda   Nov. 11, 1981
Argentina   Oct. 24, 1945
Armenia   Mar. 2, 1992
Australia   Nov. 1, 1945
Austria   Dec. 14, 1955
Azerbaijan   Mar. 2, 1992
Bahamas   Sept. 18, 1973
Bahrain   Sept. 21, 1971
Bangladesh   Sept. 17, 1974
Barbados   Dec. 9, 1966

Belarus   Oct. 24, 1945
Belgium   Dec. 27, 1945
Belize   Sept. 25, 1981
Benin   Sept. 20, 1960
Bhutan   Sept. 21, 1971
Bolivia   Nov. 14, 1945
Bosnia and Herzegovina   May 22, 1992
Botswana   Oct. 17, 1966
Brazil   Oct. 24, 1945
Brunei Darussalam   Sept. 21, 1984
Bulgaria   Dec. 14, 1955
Burkina Faso   Sept. 20, 1960
Burundi   Sept. 18, 1962
Cambodia   Dec. 14, 1955
Cameroon   Sept. 20, 1960
Canada   Nov. 9, 1945
Cape Verde   Sept. 16, 1975
Central African Republic   Sept. 20, 1960
Chad   Sept. 20, 1960
Chile   Oct. 24, 1945
China   Oct. 24, 1945
Colombia   Nov. 5, 1945
Comoros   Nov. 12, 1975
Congo (Republic of the)   Sept. 20, 1960
Costa Rica   Nov. 2, 1945
Côte d'Ivoire   Sept. 20, 1960
Croatia   May 22, 1992
Cuba   Oct. 24, 1945
Cyprus   Sept. 20, 1960
Czech Republic   Jan. 19, 1993
Democratic People's Republic of Korea   Sept. 17, 1991
Democratic Republic of the Congo   Sept. 20, 1960
Denmark   Oct. 24, 1945
Djibouti   Sept. 20, 1977
Dominica   Dec. 18, 1978

Dominican Republic   Oct. 24, 1945
Ecuador   Dec. 21, 1945
Egypt   Oct. 24, 1945
El Salvador   Oct. 24, 1945
Equatorial Guinea   Nov. 12, 1968
Eritrea   May 28, 1993
Estonia   Sept. 17, 1991
Ethiopia   Nov. 13, 1945
Fiji   Oct. 13, 1970
Finland   Dec. 14, 1955
France   Oct. 24, 1945
Gabon   Sept. 20, 1960
Gambia   Sept. 21, 1965
Georgia   July 31, 1992
Germany   Sept. 18, 1973
Ghana   Mar. 8, 1957
Greece   Oct. 25, 1945
Grenada   Sept. 17, 1974
Guatemala   Nov. 21, 1945
Guinea   Dec. 12, 1958
Guinea-Bissau   Sept. 17, 1974
Guyana   Sept. 20, 1966
Haiti   Oct. 24, 1945
Honduras   Dec. 17, 1945
Hungary   Dec. 14, 1955
Iceland   Nov. 19, 1946
India   Oct. 30, 1945
Indonesia   Sept. 28, 1950
Iran   Oct. 24, 1945
Iraq   Dec. 21, 1945
Ireland   Dec. 14, 1955
Israel   May 11, 1949
Italy   Dec. 14, 1955
Jamaica   Sept. 18, 1962
Japan   Dec. 18, 1956

Jordan   Dec. 14, 1955
Kazakhstan   Mar. 2, 1992
Kenya   Dec. 16, 1963
Kiribati   Sept. 14, 1999
Kuwait   May 14, 1963
Kyrgyzstan   Mar. 2, 1992
Lao People's Democratic Republic   Dec. 14, 1955
Latvia   Sept. 17, 1991
Lebanon   Oct. 24, 1945
Lesotho   Oct. 17, 1966
Liberia   Nov. 2, 1945
Libya   Dec. 24, 1955
Liechtenstein   Sept. 18, 1990
Lithuania   Sept. 17, 1991
Luxembourg   Oct. 24, 1945
Madagascar   Sept. 20, 1960
Malawi   Dec. 1, 1964
Malaysia   Sept. 17, 1957
Maldives   Sept. 21, 1965
Mali   Sept. 28, 1960
Malta   Dec. 1, 1964
Marshall Islands   Sept. 17, 1991
Mauritania   Oct. 27, 1961
Mauritius   Apr. 24, 1968
Mexico   Nov. 7, 1945
Micronesia (Federated States of)   Sept. 17, 1991
Monaco   May 28, 1993
Mongolia   Oct. 27, 1961
Morocco   Nov. 12, 1956
Mozambique   Sept. 16, 1975
Myanmar   Apr. 19, 1948
Namibia   Apr. 23, 1990
Nauru   Sept. 14, 1999
Nepal   Dec. 14, 1955
Netherlands   Dec. 10, 1945

New Zealand   Oct. 24, 1945
Nicaragua   Oct. 24, 1945
Niger   Sept. 20, 1960
Nigeria   Oct. 7, 1960
Norway   Nov. 27, 1945
Oman   Oct. 7, 1971
Pakistan   Sept. 30, 1947
Palau   Dec. 15, 1994
Panama   Nov. 13, 1945
Papua New Guinea   Oct. 10, 1975
Paraguay   Oct. 24, 1945
Peru   Oct. 31, 1945
Philippines   Oct. 24, 1945
Poland   Oct. 24, 1945
Portugal   Dec. 14, 1955
Qatar   Sept. 21, 1971
Republic of Korea   Sept. 17, 1991
Republic of Moldova   Mar. 2, 1992
Romania   Dec. 14, 1955
Russian Federation   Oct. 24, 1945
Rwanda   Sept. 18, 1962
Saint Kitts and Nevis   Sept. 23, 1983
Saint Lucia   Sept. 18, 1979
Saint Vincent and the Grenadines   Sept. 16, 1980
Samoa   Dec. 15, 1976
San Marino   Mar. 2, 1992
Sao Tome and Principe   Sept. 16, 1975
Saudi Arabia   Oct. 24, 1945
Senegal   Sept. 28, 1960
Seychelles   Sept. 21, 1976
Sierra Leone   Sept. 27, 1961
Singapore   Sept. 21, 1965
Slovakia   Jan. 19, 1993
Slovenia   May 22, 1992
Solomon Islands   Sept. 19, 1978

Somalia   Sept. 20, 1960
South Africa   Nov. 7, 1945
Spain   Dec. 14, 1955
Sri Lanka   Dec. 14, 1955
Sudan   Nov. 12, 1956
Suriname   Dec. 4, 1975
Swaziland   Sept. 24, 1968
Sweden   Nov. 19, 1946
Switzerland   Sept. 10, 2002
Syria   Oct. 24, 1945
Tajikistan   Mar. 2, 1992
Thailand   Dec. 16, 1946
The former Yugoslav Republic of Macedonia   Apr. 8, 1993
Timor-Leste   Sept. 27, 2002
Togo   Sept. 20, 1960
Tonga   Sept. 14, 1999
Trinidad and Tobago   Sept. 18, 1962
Tunisia   Nov. 12, 1956
Turkey   Oct. 24, 1945
Turkmenistan   Mar. 2, 1992
Tuvalu   Sept. 5, 2000
Uganda   Oct. 24, 1962
Ukraine   Oct. 24, 1945
United Arab Emirates   Dec. 9, 1971
United Kingdom   Oct. 24, 1945
United Republic of Tanzania   Dec. 14, 1961
United States   Oct. 24, 1945
Uruguay   Dec. 18, 1945
Uzbekistan   Mar. 2, 1992
Vanuatu   Sept. 15, 1981
Venezuela   Nov. 15, 1945
Vietnam   Sept. 20, 1977
Yemen   Sept. 30, 1947
Yugoslavia   Nov. 1, 2000
Zambia   Dec. 1, 1964
Zimbabwe   Aug. 25, 1980

How to Set Up a Model UN Meeting

The following is taken from *modelun@unausa.org*

The Model United Nations is a simulation of the United Nations System. In this simulation students assume the role of diplomats. They represent various countries and participate in debates about current issues in the UN agenda. Role-playing in a model UN meeting should enable you to learn:

• The concerns and hopes of people in different regions of the world;
• How people's lives worldwide can be improved through the UN;
• Skills and behavior which contribute to international cooperation.

Model UN meetings also help participants to understand the United Nations and appreciate the complexities and accomplishments of international cooperation. There are three basic components to the Model UN experience: first, an intensive preparation process researching the countries the participants represent; second, role-playing in a model UN debate where each participant assumes a role, usually that of an "ambassador" representing a country; and a final component evaluating the experience.

STEP #1: PREPARATION

The first step in a Model UN experience is to prepare yourself to be a delegate.

You will need to learn about three things:

• The country you are to represent;
• The subject or issue on the agenda;
• The work of the United Nations related to the subject or issue.

You may begin the process by doing research about the country you will represent. This particular part of the preparation is very important. You will need to know some basic facts about "your" country, which might affect its policies. Such information can be found in an up-to-date encyclopedia or a similar source. You may also want to contact the nearest diplomatic mission/embassy of the country you will represent.

Here are a few features you may want to look at: economic and political systems; social structure and values; and cultural, national, and international priorities. For example, under political, topics could include: political system today; history (former colony or former colonial power); neighbors; allies; does it belong to any regional or other grouping of nations? In what ways does your country consider the UN important?

In addition to finding factual information, you will want to try to "get inside" to see with a delegate's eyes and feel as he or she does about the world today. The objective of your research is to ascertain the ways that your country perceives the United Nations and its application to your country's interests and policies.

The country research segment of your preparation is an ongoing activity, which will take considerable time. It will also be a group effort if the Model UN you are attending requires that a delegation of several people is needed to represent a member state.

The second stage of your preparation should focus on understanding the issues or subjects that are on the Model UN's agenda. In many instances, you and your colleagues will have to deduce what your country's views may be on these matters.

A Model UN may have a singular theme, such as human rights or economic development, or it may cover several different areas of the UN's work, such as regional conflicts, disarmament, refugees, children's issues, external debt of developing countries, or the environment. Your job is to find out what your country's position or views are on these issues and to develop a strategy for the country for the Model UN session.

The last stage of your research will focus on the UN system and its work. Understanding the role and functions of the various parts of the UN system on the issues and concerns is essential to your role as a delegate. This part of your research should help you better understand the role the UN plays in international affairs and how the UN operates as a diplomatic and policy-setting body for the international community.

Once you have researched the country you will represent, the issues on the Model UN's agenda, and the UN system, you will be ready to prepare a "position paper." This should be concise, consisting of the main points you think your country would consider important for the issues to be discussed. During the simulation, you can use these points as the basis for a speech or as items you might try to have included in resolutions. As you negotiate, you will undoubtedly modify them, or you may even abandon them altogether.

STEP #2: ROLE-PLAYING

The second step in the model UN experience is applying the information and knowledge you have acquired during your preparation. Once you and the other delegates arrive either in the meeting room or at the conference facilities, you are no longer a student. You are the "official" representative of the country you have been assigned. You are a diplomat. Your purpose and that of your colleagues representing the other

UN member states is to address the issues and the problems on the agenda and to develop a workable resolution which the largest number of nations can support.

The Model UN meetings are structured by rules of procedure which provide the ways and means for countries to express their views, to consider proposals and resolutions, and to come to decisions on resolving the issues and concerns on the agenda. You will have two principal concerns:

- To express the viewpoint of the country you represent for the purpose of sharing the ideas and experience of "your" government and procuring a resolution acceptable to "your" country;
- To contribute to developing an international response fair to all nations.

Most participants in the Model UN exercise will play the roles of delegates who represent a broad spectrum of political, economic, cultural, and geographic backgrounds. If you have sufficient participants, delegations can include specialists in different areas of industrial development and environment, such as toxic wastes and hazardous chemicals.

Additional participants could play members of the press, interviewing key delegates, filing dispatches to home newspapers, etc. Others might be representatives of nongovernmental organizations (NGOs) invited as observers.

You should also invite a knowledgeable person to observe and comment on the meeting. Best would be someone who has worked for the UN or on a national delegation to a meeting at the United Nations. To role-play well will require serious research—and imagination. You will need to be a skillful diplomat, aware of your nation's priorities, but flexible, sensitive to other's viewpoints, and willing to work for consensus and the common good.

Role-playing involves working in a group and making speeches. As soon as you begin the meetings, you will want to meet informally with delegates of countries with backgrounds and concerns similar to yours in order to coordinate ideas and actions. In the Model UN these groups are often called "caucus groups." These groups are all un-official and are not bodies that can bind "your" country to any position or viewpoint. The purpose of these groups is to facilitate the negotiating process. For example, the developing countries have formed the "Group of 77," which concentrates on forming a common agenda among over 130 countries in Africa, Asia, Latin America, and the Middle East. Similarly, most western European countries are now grouped under the European Union (EU).

Negotiations are very intense and can be very frustrating, especially in the larger groups. Most of the diplomatic work is accomplished during the informal caucuses producing draft resolutions, amend-ments, and the important compromises needed to reach consensus.

Speech-making during formal proceedings is another important part of role-playing. These public pronouncements permit delegates to "show their stuff" as orators and thinkers to the rest of the group. Yet not everyone is a polished speaker, and in the Model UN debate, substance is as important as the style at the podium. A careful balance of listening and speaking must be struck in order to generate support and to find consensus on the problem.

The end result of the process is the adoption of a resolution or resolu-tions by a vote, reflecting the aggregate of interests of the member states at the meeting. Therefore, your purpose at the Model UN is not to make the best presentation or to have "your" resolution win. Suc-cessful diplomacy is reaching a consensus on a resolution or proposal.

STEP #3: EVALUATION

Once the simulation is over, you should evaluate what you have learned from the experience. Here are some ways you might want to do this.

- What did the meeting accomplish from the point view of the coun-try you represented?
- How closely did the Model UN simulate the real UN?

As your country's representative you would report to your Ministry of Foreign Affairs. Write such a report, include your evaluation of

whether the resolution passed included points considered important
by "your" country, whether they did not include such points but were
nonetheless acceptable, or whether they were unacceptable. You may
also add your suggestions on what actions your country might take to
carry out the resolutions.

You and [your] colleagues should also discuss whether the simulation accurately reflected the situation in the world and in the UN
today. An attempt should be made to explain what the main obstacles
to agreements were and how such obstacles could have been over-
come. Finally you might want to analyze how the real delegates at the
UN addressed the same issue by looking at UN documents and resolutions on these issues.

From start to finish, the Model UN experience is an excellent way
to learn about the United Nations and international relations. The
world's issues and concerns actually come alive and you are at the
center of it all. All it takes is dedication and enthusiasm to be a part of
the ultimate diplomatic experience.

FOR FURTHER READING

- *Basic Facts about the United Nations.* This book provides a general
  introduction to the role and functions of the United Nations and its
  related agencies. Very helpful for students at secondary and higher
  levels. Copies should be ordered through UN Publications.
- *Everything You Always Wanted to Know about the United Nations.* A
  question and answer book, written for students at intermediate and
  secondary levels. For copies, write to the Public Inquiries Unit.
- Annotated preliminary list of items in the provisional agenda of the
  General Assembly. Issued every year prior to the beginning of the
  UN General Assembly. A must for all Model UN participants. For
  copies, write to UN Publications.
- *The Model UN Survival Kit.* Contains four publications, which provide comprehensive information for students and faculty participat-
  ing in a Model UN. Issued annually by UNA-USA.
- *Model UN Security Council Kit.* A simulation package designed for
  use in the classroom and as a community program activity. A UNA-
  USA publication.

If you want to place an order for a UN publication listed above, please write to UN Publications, 2 UN Plaza, Room DC2–853, New York, NY 10017. Tel (212) 963–8302; Fax (212) 963–3489; e-mail: *publications@un.org*

For further inquiries, contact: Public Inquiries, GA-57, United Nations, NY 10017. Fax (212) 963–0071; e-mail: *inquiries@un.org*

For more information regarding Model UN conferences, please contact Lucia Rodriguez, Executive Director, Education and Model U.N., UNA-USA, 801 Second Avenue, 2nd Floor, New York, NY 10017, *modelun@unausa.org*

The sources for this book are available in libraries and on the Internet, except for the interviews that I conducted with diplomats, UN officials, scholars, and the like. Unless otherwise noted in the text, all quotations in the book come from these interviews.

For basic information about the UN system I relied heavily on the websites of the UN and its various organs, agencies, commissions, and programs. I also consulted the standard reference work by the UN, *Basic Facts about the United Nations* (New York: United Nations, 2000). Three US State Department reports, available on the State Department's website (*www.state.gov*), provided detailed information about important aspects of the UN. The first is the *US Report to the UN Counterterrorism Committee*, December 19, 2001, which describes the US government's actions taken in compliance with Security Council resolution 1373, against terrorism. The second is the *18th Annual Report on Voting Practices in the UN*, 2000, which analyzes how UN member states voted in comparison with US voting patterns. The third, *US Participation in the United Nations*, 2000, minutely describes the relationship of the US with all parts of the UN system, including financial assessments and contributions.

I used the United Nations Foundation's website to access UNWire, an electronic database that contains English-language news stories about the UN for about the past three years. The entries provide summaries and in many cases full text of the articles. I have not referenced UNWire at each point where I used it, but I acknowledge here that it was an invaluable tool. In those instances where I quoted from or relied heavily on news stories, these are noted below, by chapter, in the order in which they appear.

Chapter 3.   Newton Bowles, *Diplomacy of Hope*, provided information on UNAMIR and General Romeo Dallaire in Rwanda. David Malone, in a letter to the *Toronto Star*, Jan. 5, 2000, praised Annan for commissioning the report on the Rwanda genocide.

Chapter 11.   US pleasure at the creation of the Office of Internal Oversight Services is expressed in the State Department report *US Participation in the UN*, 2000, p. 119; it describes the results-based budgeting initiative on p. 55. The GAO report, *United Nations Reform Initiatives Have Strengthened Operations, But Overall Objectives Have Not Yet Been Achieved*, was published in May 2000. Barbara Crossette's *New York Times* story on it (May 29) is presented in UNWire, May 31, 2000. The UNICEF quotation is from Reshma Prakash's story in the *Earth Times*, Oct. 4, 1999. The mess at UNESCO is presented in articles by Jon Henley of the *London Guardian*, Oct. 18 and 20, 1999; *Agence France-Presse*, Oct. 18, 1999; and Michael Binyon, *Times* (London), Aug. 8, 2000.

Chapter 12.   The "unprecedented act" by the US is described in the State Department's report *US Participation in the UN*, 2000, pp. 112–13. The debate about the outreach to the corporate world is in UNWire, summarizing stories by Patricia Lumiell in the *Washington Times*, Mar. 13, 1999, Joan Oleck in *Business Week*, Mar. 22, 1999; and in UNWire, Sept. 6, 2000. The Adopt-A-Minefield program is described by Kevin Newman of ABC in UNWire, Dec. 10, 1999.

Chapter 18.   The data on the proliferation of NGOs comes from Curtis Runyan, *World Watch*, November/December 1999.

Chapter 21.   The report criticizing traditional development was issued by the UNDP and is summarized in UNWire, Apr. 5, 2000.

Chapter 23.   See the story about Carol Bellamy by Barbara Crossette, "From City Hall to the World's Stage," *New York Times*, Apr. 22, 2002.

Chapter 26.   Prime Minister Fini was quoted in *Corriere della Serra*, Mar. 15, 2002, translated by UNWire. The UNDCP's director of youth programs, Stefano Berterami, was quoted in *Corriere della Serra*, Mar. 13, 2002, translated by UNWire.

The appendixes are drawn from the UN's Office of Public Inquiries.

UN and Other Websites

UN Homepage: *www.un.org*
UN Main Bodies: *www.un.org/aboutun/mainbodies.htm*
UN News: *www.un.org/news*
UN NGOs: *www.un.org/esa/coordination/ngo/*
UN Organization Website Locator: *www.unsystem.org*
UN Permanent Missions: *www.un.it*

Better World Campaign: *www.betterworldfund.org*
Center on International Cooperation: *www.cic.nyu.edu*
Council on Foreign Relations: *www.cfr.org*
Foreign Policy Association: *www.fpa.org*
International Crisis Group: *www.intl-crisis-group.org*
International Peace Academy: *www.ipacademy.org*
Model UN: *modelun@unausa.org*
UN Association of the United States: *www.unausa.org*
UN Foundation: *www.unfoundation.org*
UN Wire: *www.unwire.org*
US State Department: *www.state.gov*
World Affairs Councils of America: *www.worldaffairscouncils.org*

General

Annan, Kofi A. *We the Peoples: The Role of the United Nations in the 21st Century.* New York: United Nations, 2000.

Boutros-Ghali, B. *Unvanquished: A US-UN Saga.* New York: Random House, 1999.

Bowles, N. R. *The Diplomacy of Hope: The United Nations Since the Cold War.* Ottawa, Canada: United Nations Association in Canada, 2001.

Emmerij, L., and R. Jolly. *Ahead of the Curve?: UN Ideas and Global Challenges.* Bloomington: Indiana University Press, 2001.

Gorman, R. F. *Great Debates at the United Nations: An Encyclopedia of Fifty Key Issues, 1945–2000.* Westport, Conn.: Greenwood Publishing, 2001.

Hoopes, T. *FDR and the Creation of the United Nations.* New Haven: Yale University Press, 2000.

Luard, E. *The United Nations: How It Works and What It Does.* New York: St. Martin's Press, 1994.

Malone, David M., and Y. F. Khong, eds. *Unilateralism and U.S. Foreign Policy: International Perspectives.* Boulder, Colo.: Lynne Rienner Publishers, 2003.

Mingst, K. A., and M. P. Karns. *The United Nations in The Post–Cold War Era,* 2nd edition. Boulder, Colo.: Westview Press, 2000.

New Zealand Ministry of Foreign Affairs. *United Nations Handbook: 2001.* Wellington, New Zealand: New Zealand Ministry of Foreign Affairs and Trade, 2001.

Patrick, S., and S. Forman. *Multilateralism and US Foreign Policy: Ambivalent Engagement.* Boulder, Colo.: Lynne Rienner Publishers, 2002.

Ruggie, John Gerard, ed. *Constructing World Polity: Essays on International Institutionalization.* London: Routledge, 1998.

——. *Multilateralism Matters: The Theory and Praxis of an Institutional Form.* New York: Columbia University Press, 1993.

Russett, Bruce, ed. *The Once and Future Security Council.* New York: St. Martin's Press, 1997.

Sutterlin, James S. *The United Nations and the Maintenance of International Security: A Challenge to Be Met.* Westport, Conn.: Praeger, 1995.

Taylor, P., and A. J. R. Groom. *The United Nations at the Millennium: The Principal Organs.* New York: Continuum, 2000.

Tesner, S. *The United Nations and Business: A Partnership Recovered.* New York: Palgrave Macmillan, 2000. *http://unbisnet.un.org/newacq/toc/627403.pdf*

United Nations. *Basic Facts About the United Nations.* New York: United Nations, 2000.

US Department of State, *www.state.gov. US Participation in the UN, Yearly Reports.* 1990–2000.

——. *18th Annual Report on Voting Practices in the UN,* 2000.

——. *US Report to the UN Counterterrorism Committee,* December 19, 2001.

Weiss, T. G., and D. P. Forsythe. *The United Nations and Changing World Politics.* Boulder, Colo.: Westview Press, 2001.

Humanitarian Aid

Forman, S., and S. Patrick, eds. *Good Intentions: Pledges of Aid for Post-Conflict Recovery.* Boulder, Colo.: Lynne Rienner Publishers, 2000.

Helton, A. C. *The Price of Indifference: Refugees and Humanitarian Action in the New Century.* Oxford: Oxford University Press, 2002.

Shaw, D. J. *The UN World Food Programme and the Development of Food Aid.* New York: Palgrave Macmillan, 2001. *http://unbisnet.un.org/newacq/toc/666373.pdf*

Human Rights

Glendon, M. A. A. *World Made New: Eleanor Roosevelt and the Universal Declaration of Human Rights.* New York: Random House, 2001.

Human Rights Watch. *World Report: Human Rights Watch.* New York: Human Rights Watch, annual.

Power, S., and G. Allison. *Realizing Human Rights: Moving from Inspiration to Impact.* New York: St. Martin's Press, 2000.

Schoenberg, H. O. *The World Conference Against Racism: The Adoption and Repeal of the Z=R Resolution and the Implications for UN Reform.* Wayne, N.J.: Centre for United Nations Reform Education, 2001.

United Nations. *Human Rights Today: A United Nations Priority.* New York: United Nations, 1998.

Peace and Peacekeeping

Annan, Kofi A. *Prevention of Armed Conflict: Report of the Secretary-General.* New York: United Nations, 2002.

Barnett, M. *Eyewitness to a Genocide: The United Nations and Rwanda.* Ithaca, N.Y.: Cornell University Press, 2002.

Berdal, M., and D. Malone, eds. *Greed and Grievance: Economic Agendas in Civil Wars.* Boulder, Colo.: Lynne Rienner Publishers, 2000.

Boulden, J. *Peace Enforcement: The United Nations Experience in Congo, Somalia, and Bosnia.* New York: Praeger Publishing, 2001.

Chesterman, S. *East Timor in Transition: From Conflict Prevention to State-Building.* New York: International Peace Academy, 2001.

Cortright, D., and G. Lopez. *Sanctions and the Search for Security: Challenges to UN Action.* Boulder, Colo.: Lynne Rienner Publishers, 2002.

Cousens, E. M., and C. K. Cater. *Toward Peace in Bosnia: Implementing the Dayton Accords.* Boulder, Colo.: Lynne Rienner Publishers, 2001.

Cousens, E. M., and C. Kumar. *Peacebuilding as Politics: Cultivating Peace in Fragile Societies.* Boulder, Colo.: Lynne Rienner Publishers, 2001.

Durch, William J., ed. *The Evolution of UN Peacekeeping: Case Studies and Comparative Analysis.* New York: St. Martin's Press, 1993.

Haass, Richard N., ed. *Economic Sanctions and American Diplomacy.* New York: Council on Foreign Relations, 1998.

Hampson, F. O., and D. Malone. *From Reaction to Conflict Prevention: Opportunities for the UN System.* Boulder, Colo.: Lynne Rienner Publishers, 2002.

Hirsch, J., and R. Oakley. *Somalia & Operation Restore Hope: Reflections on Peacemaking & Peacekeeping.* Washington, D.C.: U.S. Institute of Peace Press, 1995.

International Development Research Centre. *The Responsibility to Protect: Report of the International Commission on Intervention and State Sovereignty.* Ottawa, Canada: International Development Research Centre, December 2001.

Jones, B. D. *Peacemaking in Rwanda: The Dynamics of Failure.* Boulder, Colo.: Lynne Rienner Publishers, 2001.

Khan, S. M. *The Shallow Graves of Rwanda.* London: I B Tauris & Co Ltd, 2001.

Luck, E. C. *Mixed Messages: American Politics and International Organization, 1919–1999.* Washington, D.C.: Brookings Institution Press, 1999.

Machel, G. *The Impact of the War on Children: A Review of Progress Since the 1996 United Nations Report on the Impact of Armed Conflict on Children.* New York: Palgrave Macmillan, 2001.

MacKinnon, M. G. *The Evolution of US Peacekeeping Policy Under Clinton: A Fairweather Friend?* London: Frank Cass & Co., 2000.

Martin, I. *Self-determination in East Timor: The United Nations, the Ballot, and the International Intervention.* Boulder, Colo.: Lynne Rienner Publishers, 2001.

Martin, L. *Democratic Commitments: Legislatures and International Cooperation.* Princeton, N.J.: Princeton University Press, 2000.

Ould-Ablallah, A. *Burundi on the Brink, 1993–95: A UN Special Envoy Reflects on Preventive Diplomacy.* Washington, D.C.: United States Institute of Peace, 2000.

Rikhye, I. *The Politics and Practice of United Nations Peacekeeping: Past, Present and Future.* Cornwallis, N.S.: Canadian Peacekeeping Press, 2000.

Shawcross, William. *Deliver Us from Evil: Peacekeepers, Warlords and World of Endless Conflict.* New York: Simon & Schuster, 2000.

United Nations. *An Agenda for Peace: Preventive Diplomacy, Peacemaking and Peacekeeping.* A/47/277-S/24111, 17 June 1992. Full text available at http://www.un.org/Docs/SG/agpeace.html

——. "Report of the Panel on United Nations Peace Operations," A/55/305, S/2000/809, 2000. Full text available at http://www.un.org/peace/reports/peace_operations/

——. *UN Peacekeeping: 50 Years (1948–1998).* New York: United Nations, 1998.

United Nations Association of the United States. *The Preparedness Gap: Making Peace Operations Work in the 21st Century: A Policy Report of the United Nations Association of the United States of America.* New York: United Nations Association of the United States, 2000.

INDEX

Page numbers in *italic* indicate illustrations.

Academic Council on the United Nations System (ACUNS), 143–44
Administrative Committee on Coordination, 159
Adopt-A-Minefield campaign, 142
Afghanistan, 72, 81, 89, 110, 200–201
Agencies, 4, 7, 93, 158–60; budget, 71; directors of, 112; lack of field coordination, 108. *See also* Bureaucracy
Agenda, 21, 178–79
AIDS crisis, 46, 76, 177
Albright, Madeleine, 10, 13, *35*, 35, 36, 41–42, 93, 108, 135, 166

Alternative Development Program, 198, *199*, 201
Annan, Kofi, xii, 1, 3–4, *20*, *28*, 31, 57, *80*, *121*, *140*, 148, 160, 178, 191; candidacy for Secretary General, 137; on development, 27, 170; on digital divide, 192–93; effective leadership of, 17, 20, 28–30, 137; Global Compact and, 194; human rights approach of, 23–28, 161, 164–65; on partnerships, 139, 156; peacekeeping and, 25–26, 59, 60, 62; personal history of, 18–19; reforms of, 21, 23, 107–8; on terrorism, 79; on UN headquarters renovation, 133
Annan, Nane Lagergren, 19, *20*, *140*

237